Blackberry Season

A Time to Mourn, A Time to Heal

H. H. PRICE

San Diego, California

LuraMedia™

Cover image and section title page art by Sara Steele.
Four panels from "One Through Seven,"
© Copyright 1986 by Sara Steele. All Rights Reserved.

Cover design by Tom Jackson, Philadelphia.

Library of Congress Cataloging-in-Publication Data

Price, H.H. (Harriet H.), date.
Blackberry season : a time to mourn, a time to heal / H.H. Price
p.   cm.
ISBN 0-931055-93-8
1. Price, H.H. (Harriet H.), date. 2. Loss (Psychology)--Vermont--Case studies.
3. Interpersonal relations--Vermont--Case studies.
4. Loss (Psychology)--United States--Case studies.
I. Interpersonal relations--United States--Case studies. I. Title.
BF575.D35P75   1993
973.92'092–dc20   92-44882
[B]   CIP

"The Spring House" originally appeared in *Vermont Life*, Spring 1985.
"Country Medicine" originally appeared in *Gourmet*, October 1987.

Excerpt from "The Pasture" by Robert Frost
from THE POEMS OF ROBERT FROST
edited by Edward Connery Lathem
is reprinted by permission of Henry Holt and Company, Inc.

for Mattie, who is always with me

To every thing there is a season,
and a time to every purpose under the heaven:

A time to be born, and a time to die;
a time to plant, and a time to pluck up that which is planted;

A time to kill, and a time to heal;
a time to break down, and a time to build up;

A time to weep, and a time to laugh;
a time to mourn, and a time to dance;

A time to cast away stones, and a time to gather stones together;
a time to embrace, and a time to refrain from embracing;

A time to get, and a time to lose;
a time to keep, and a time to cast away;

A time to rend, and a time to sew;
a time to keep silence, and a time to speak;

A time to love, and a time to hate;
a time of war, and a time of peace.

Ecclesiastes 3:1-8
KJV

Contents

□

Introduction

The stories in *Blackberry Season* are stepping-stones across the landscape of my life like a path of rocks that leads across a shallow creek or a wet pasture. They begin in 1947 when I am seven years old and have lost my mother, and end when I am almost fifty and have finally reckoned with my loss. My mother had not died in 1947; she had broken down and become a mental health patient. Her illness lasted for forty years that were equally divided among mental institutions, living on her own, and, in the end, nursing homes. So, she rarely appears in person in *Blackberry Season*. However, she highlights each story — each stepping-stone — as if she were the black ink in a drawing that outlines or underlines the stones, or she were the shadowing in a painting of me stepping on the stones. My mother's absence, or lack of visibility, colored everything in life for me.

It was blackberry season in 1947 when my mother was "put away" and my fourteen-year-old brother, my only sibling, and I were taken in by our paternal grandparents who lived on a small subsistence farm in their ancestral Vermont village. Their way of life, which in post-World War II was not much different than before World War I, is what I call "country medicine," and I lapped it up like a calf at a salt lick. Our father was working in another state, so we only saw him on the weekends when he could make the trip to the farm. We looked forward to his visits with the expectation that our family would soon be reunited. However, Dad's short visits were taken up with disciplining my brother, who had been unruly in his absence, and then suddenly Dad was gone.

His visits resurrected the internal unseen chaos instead of reinstating order. In retrospect, I know our nuclear family was tearing apart at the seams so fast one could almost hear them rip.

Initially, I did not mind the breakup of my family because I felt secure in my grandparents' care. However, that did not last long. A few months after we went to live with our grandparents, Grampa died. Grampa was the one with the prescription for good living. He started with himself and was as good a man as I have ever known, except the one I married. The great rock upon which our extended family leaned was gone.

Everyone was affected in some way by Grampa's death, but my brother, whom Grampa might have tamed had he lived, just bolted from the farm like a wild colt breaking through a corral gate. He began a lifelong pattern of running away, looking for greener pastures after our family pasture had suffered such a drought. He would return to wherever our father had relocated, then would bolt again, and the cycle would begin anew. He never stayed on one of my "stepping-stones" long enough to be included in these stories, so he appears only in the beginning on the day we lost our mother. *Blackberry Season* is about my loss, not about my brother's.

After Grampa died, Gramma and I simply had to knuckle down to what life had dealt us. Our losses were so great that, like a bankrupt business or a failed farm, we started over totally anew. My grandparents' way of life gave me the necessary prescriptions to start again, and luckily I was in their intensive care during a critical few months at a crucial age. The cure took hold without my even knowing I needed it.

My grandmother and I stuck together through those first tough years until I was about ten, living wherever my Dad was working. Gramma set up housekeeping in one city apartment after another, and I took on several schools in waves of meeting new friends and then saying good-bye almost as soon as we had met. Finally, when we moved to the Midwest, my grandmother awakened, I suppose, to her own grief, and she could come to terms with life without Grampa only by going back to their ancestral village. So she left me with my father halfway across the country, and, as I look back, I experienced a second maternal abandonment, which began my long journey across the remaining stones alone. It was my time for reckoning with what I had missed and would never get back: my mother.

While I was "reckoning," my mother was facing mental health treatments that were diminishing instead of restorative, so we grew irretrievably apart. Yet — and I wish she knew — I yearned so much for her that I both forgot about her and thought constantly about her at the same time. Since she was not with me, she was always with me. I could not let her go. My loss of mother completely shaped my life; and, as a parent now, I imagine her loss of children broke her heart.

I eventually reckoned with my loss, which is the subject of this book. I gradually found "mothering" in nature, human nature, images, symbols, religion, and a sense of belonging to a place — Vermont — and the surrogates became my healing. Something happened in the process, and I do not know which came first: I either let go of the dream that my mother would mother me so there was room for the replacements, or the nurturing I found helped me let the dream go.

There is a mystery to the process: What I thought were insurmountable hurdles to be jumped or skipped over, faded as I healed. The exchange, or the transformation, took place in these stories in the darkness of berry bushes, a spring of water, a rare flower, and the moon; in a "Mama Cat," Gramma's song, a mother tongue, my cousin "Mama Dear," "Mother Nature," and a Gothic cathedral; in a mirror, a homemade book, a table, and on a shelf in my grandfather's "medicine chest"; and, finally, deep within myself.

Each story highlights some natural healing element, such as clean water, good food, sunlight, storytelling, memories, rest, and laughter, or some comforting aspect of human nature; or, as I matured, some sign or symbol. The stories, although presented in chronological order, weave back and forth in time and draw on images that may evoke the reader's own images. They were decades in the making and ten years in writing down, as time wove carefully the threads of my life and bound the wound. I invite the reader to keep me company as I walk across the stepping-stones of what I now realize was the greenest of all pastures for me.

B L A C K B E R R Y   S E A S O N

I.

Country Medicine

A Time to Lose, A Time to Gain

□ □ □ □

CHAPTER 1

Blackberry Season

When blackberries hang heavily from their wild and wandering thorny branches, I relive the day I lost my mother. Should I be berrying and overturn a morning's worth of picking, all collected in a bucket or a big basket, I have a sudden image of my loss. I peer through the dark brambles at the waste and feel the emptiness from my childhood.

This overturning of my family bucket happened forty years ago. I was seven years old, a skinny little pale-faced girl with two brown ponytails pulled off my forehead, and my brother, tanned darkly from the sun, was exactly twice my age and size that summer. Our father, who was working in New Hampshire, had just farmed us out to his parents in Vermont because our mother was irrational, angry, and, as it turned out, breaking down. Our grandparents lived on a small subsistence farm at the outskirts of the dairy village where they had always been. They immediately began pouring "country medicine" into me, although I did not understand that at the time. Their Vermont style of healing began in blackberry season on the day my mother disappeared from me, and I recall clearly how it started.

My brother shot across the worn-down yard between the barn and the house and headed toward the town road with a bucket dangling from each gangly arm.

"Where you goin'?" Gramma shouted from the porch. Just as soon as she caught sight of my brother walking away, she ran from the hot woodburning kitchen stove to the end of the long screened-in porch that hung over the backyard. If I should name Gramma's kitchen as the sanctuary of our lives and her cast-iron cookstove as its altar, the porch would be the sacristy. It had a wooden icebox, a butter churn, milk pails and pans, a squeaky iron swinging couch, old wicker rocking chairs, and a large, worn, gray rag rug. There was ample space for storing harvest fruits and vegetables, until Gramma could "put them by," and for cousins to giggle and make up games.

"You can't take off just like that," Gramma reprimanded my brother.

"I'm goin' blackberrin'," he said without looking back. "For the day," he shouted to close the conversation.

"The bugs will eatcha alive," Gramma began to reason. "Oh, Son, it's too hot today," she said as she wiped the bottom of her apron along her perspiring forehead. Then Gramma saw she could not draw him back because he kept walking while she was reasoning. "You wait," she said kindly. "I'll fix you a sandwich and something cool to drink. And I'll make jelly from whatever you bring back."

"I had a pie or two in mind," he said sullenly. Yet he broke his stride.

"All right, all right," Gramma acquiesced.

My brother headed down the road with lunch in his buckets. I could tell he was angry by the way he threw the buckets back and forth in syncopated measure with his steps, flinging them as far apart and with as hard a swing as a pendulum can go. Whenever he was angry or saw trouble brewing up ahead, he took off to fish or berry-pick with no thought to ask permission, as if he were a weather vane turning before the full change in wind. I knew where he was going, if he intended to pick enough for both pies and jelly. The great storehouse of blackberries in the village grew in profusion along the back of the cemetery where the mowed slope met the wild woods, a kind of thicket for our ancestors. One could look over the green valley and the village and the distant hills and mountains from the great blackberry thicket, but I imagine my brother stuck to business and did not waste his time gazing at the scenery.

There were changes both in the outside weather and in the farmhouse atmosphere that day. Even now as a grown woman, when I am hanging laundry on the line in late August, I am reminded of the fateful day. The prevailing winds suddenly turn. Shadows begin to replace highlights around the old maple trees. Stream waters barely make a sound. That seasonal switch blows my memory back to August, 1947, when I saw and heard domestic changes taking place inside my grandparents' home.

The old-fashioned brown box crank telephone on the wall beneath the stairs in the parlor kept ringing that day: two shorts, one long, or other combinations of longs and shorts. It was a most unusual din for a farmhouse in the 1940s. On that August day, Gramma cranked the lever to raise the operator to phone out and raised her voice and cheek color as she worked on a mysterious problem. She brushed strands off her forehead toward her full head of gray hair twisted in a bun like a skein of flaxen linen and shifted her full body in the straight chair with each call — to the left for calls "in" and to the right for calls "out." It was not Sunday, but Gramma had donned a printed cotton dress she would normally wear for church. Grampa came in from the barn or thereabouts and changed from overalls and boots to cotton slacks and a dress shirt. He planted himself in a green wicker chair beside the large parlor fern and, although it was August and hot, he wrapped a deep purple shawl around his shoulders. He scolded Gramma, which was as much out of character for him as his sitting still.

"I want no part of this," Grampa said stubbornly. "We shouldn't get mixed up in this domestic broil."

"I want the children here," she snapped at him. "Their father can't take care of them alone and their mother shouldn't. We'd be best for them. I'm calling a halt to these shenanigans."

The more they argued, the more I got underfoot. I was such a small tyke, with skinny arms and legs poking through a sleeveless shirt and shorts, that I must have thought they would not notice me. I hung onto Grampa's chair, and then I slipped across the parlor on scattered rugs to hang onto Gramma's chair. Suddenly, her hand fell upon my shoulder.

"Now, Peanut," she said. "You'll have to go upstairs. You haven't been bad, so don't think that. I just need you out of the way right now."

Although it was nowhere near the time to nap, Gramma settled me on a cot beside an upstairs window in the bedroom she and Grampa shared. The room was sparse but colorful with dark green-painted floors and a rag rug to match, pink-and-white-flowered paper on the walls, and a golden bird's-eye maple double bed covered with one of Gramma's quilts. I could see over the back porch roof to Grampa's square, two-story, sand-colored brick barn surrounded by pens and gardens, and then beyond to fenced-in pastures that rolled down to maple trees along the creek. The railroad track etched beside the creek's bank, and I saw and heard freight trains pass twice that day, as if making a sure impression on a steel engraving of the landscape. Green pastures rose on the other side of the creek to meet a blue-washed sky. Red barns and tall hardwoods stood along the horizon like a stand of straight sentries, natural guards around my world. I could see over Grampa's barn roof to the center of the village where little houses clustered around a bridge, a big yellow schoolhouse, and two steepled churches.

First I heard muffled voices through the porch roof, and then I heard Gramma's voice come up through the floor register. She was right beneath me in the kitchen at the back door.

"No, you can't come in. I don't care who you came for," she shouted as she slammed the door. She struggled against someone to set the bolt in place. I knew Gramma was strong from lugging laundry baskets and iron pots and from scrubbing everything by hand, but I imagined she was most forceful with her eyes when she stared through the door window at her adversary.

Then I heard my mother's voice. Gramma had locked her out as surely as she closed glass canning jars with a metal snap. I did not know how my mother had gotten to the farm, so far from home, but I knew why she had come — to take me home.

Two weeks earlier my mother had tried to keep me at home with her words, shouted from the steps at our side door. My father and brother had packed in a sudden flurry to leave, and I had watched them load the car while I sat in the swing. As they backed out of the driveway, I could not tell if they were going on a holiday or leaving permanently. I ran after the car, hung on to its door handle, and begged to go with them.

"They'll be back, Harriet," my mother had shouted to me as my father was deciding whether or not to let me in the car. "You stay home with me," my mother coaxed me.

There had been a tug of war between my parents about whether I should stay or go, and my father had won by opening his door, letting me in the back seat, and quickly backing up the car. My mother's final words to me, as I waved a weak good-bye to her from the oval back-seat car window, rang in my ears that afternoon as I sat on the cot in the upstairs bedroom of my grandparents' farmhouse: "You'll be back. I'll come and get you if I have to." Those were the last sane words I heard my mother say for many years.

My mother's garbled sentences and screams from my grandparents' back porch made no sense. Something had gone awry for her like a heaved slab of granite slipping from a foundation, and our family life crumbled with the shift. It was madness.

She had come to get me, but she would not find me on the upstairs cot unless I yelled down to her or she broke through Gramma's locked door. I was too unsettled, too frightened, to go to her, and Gramma was too determined to keep her out. My mother just rooted on the porch all day where she joined the vigil of the icebox and the butter churn, and Grampa stayed in the parlor while Gramma cranked the phone. It was a standoff between my mother and her in-laws while my father was away, my brother berry-picked, and I brooded on the upstairs cot.

No child is able to decipher adult arguments, so I fantasized about picking blackberries instead of paying careful attention to the day's quarrels. The bedroom was hot, and the fighting made me perspire. I imagined myself outside, swimming with my cousins in the cool creek or berry-picking like my brother. I looked out the window at the same view he would have had from the cemetery thicket and pretended that I had gone "a-berrin" in overalls, a long-sleeved shirt, and a 'kerchief on my head. Gramma would have given me a small pail and a jam sandwich, too.

. . . . I pretend I am plucking a few berries on the brambles' edge and snitch one for every two that drop into the pail. Then I look through the wild thorny bushes to a darkness where I know the best ones grow. The leaves are sparse on thick but brittle-looking red-brown branches and seem too little company for such big clumps of berries. I am surrounded by the maze and look up to see red and purple sparkles on little black baskets in midair — tiny pinheads of light shining in the forest. They are hanging from a knot of vines wound around a tree branch way above my head, and I reach to pick them.

"Snap!" The not-so-brittle vine, resilient with a load of shiny baskets, pulls back, and I lose the bunch but gain some scratches on my neck. The brambles wind around my feet as I push through the thorny berry patch in an obsession to fill my pail with the little black baskets without handles, and I know my hands will itch for days . . . .

"Snap," I heard and awoke from my reverie. I looked out the window to a strange car sitting in the barnyard.

"Oh, I hope it's Daddy," I said aloud, kneeling on the cot and clasping my hands together. "When's he goin' a come and make this right?"

My father was a peaceful sort of person, calm like watercress growing in a rushing stream. I thought he could sort out Grampa's argument with Gramma or be company for my mother on the back porch.

It was not my father. I saw two men shutting the car doors. They were dressed in uniforms. Suddenly, like an awakened cat, my mother began to screech. I heard thuds against the house and the sound of broken glass. The porch door at the top of the long, outside stairway kept slamming. The men shouted and cursed. There was wrestling which finally gave way to a less torpid time, but the telephone still rang our combination like a fire alarm repeated until the fire is squelched. It was strange clamor for a farmhouse: that haven of routine and good food; and the noise was as disturbing as the roar of swarming bees. My mother was in the thick of it like the waning queen bee in a divided hive, and I did not go to her.

The uproar suddenly emptied out with a final wrestle, one scream, a single slam of a door, and a whip of thuds down the outside stairs that sounded like a rolling pin run across a washboard. I dared to look out the window, and it is well I did. I saw my mother at the very end of her freedom. The two men had tied her hands and were holding her like a prisoner. They pushed my mother, who was wearing a light blue dress and silk stockings and high heels, into the car's back seat as if they were packing without folding for a last-minute trip. They drove away from the farmhouse and the din disappeared. Gramma came upstairs immediately.

"I'm sorry for you, Peanut," she said as she stroked my hair, which was wet from perspiring. "It was the only thing to do. You come downstairs now, little one. Grampa needs you in the barn to feed the calf. I'll fix supper."

We looked for my brother to come home with his full buckets. He crossed the road with a heavy burden hanging from each gangly arm, and his stride looked like a pendulum slowing to a stop. He was about as proud of his berry-picking as of any other youthful feat. That evening we ate blackberries and bread and milk for supper as if we were all Peter Rabbit's siblings, and the next day we had pie for dinner. Gramma simmered a batch of berries on the wood cookstove and dripped the midnight-colored juice into a milk pan on the back porch. She had her makings for a deep purple jelly in sparkling glasses, which we would bring up from the cellar for a winter treat.

My family bucket was overturned that day and emptied out forever as surely as a basketful of blackberries that spill into the bushes' brambles can never be retrieved. My mother was so ill I did not see her again until I was sixteen years old. Her illness affected all of us the way a plague or a war can destroy a family. My father worked away. My brother ran away. Grampa may have tightened up or worked too hard because his heart gave out when that autumn turned to winter. Gramma just went on in her maternal country fashion and kept routine, good food to eat, and me.

□ □ □ □

CHAPTER 2

The Springhouse

When my father returned to his parents' farm on weekends, he often checked the Sheldon village spring. My memory of the experience is straight from the poem "The Pasture" by Robert Frost:

> I'm going out to clean the pasture spring;
> I'll only stop to rake the leaves away
> (And wait to watch the water clear, I may):
> I sha'n't be gone long. — You come too.

> I'm going out to fetch the little calf
> That's standing by the mother. It's so young,
> It totters when she licks it with her tongue.
> I sha'n't be gone long. — You come too.

It was a morning's hike, to and from the spring, if one walked up behind the village, across the pasture and past all its fences, to where the rising slope met the dark green woods. Perhaps still feeling the city pace, Dad always drove instead. We bumped over a rutty dirt road in his black Ford until the field took over, then picked our way by foot to the springhouse.

As I look back, he was not dressed for country work when we went to the springhouse. He wore gray flannels, shiny from sitting, and a long-sleeved white shirt, which he rolled up at the sleeves as we approached the spring. His father did the business differently. He dressed in overalls and boots — farmer's garb — and crossed the pasture by foot "to rake the leaves away"; but Grampa's ways, I now realize, would soon be gone.

The springhouse was long and low and gray, a kind of wood-shingled tent. It looked as if someone had taken the attic peak of a house, sawed it off at the eaves, and laid it over the spring. On one end was a little door, just my size, that Dad tugged at to fight the swell of the wood. My job was to hand him the crowbar the moment he worked up a crack. Inside, it was dark except for the shaft of light from the little door propped ajar. The floor was wood planking with a wide trap door set in the middle.

Like desert people worshipping an oasis, Dad and I knelt carefully beside the trap door as he started to lift it. "Back up now," he cautioned me. "Be careful. Move back. I can't worry about your falling in."

Normally, Dad was a patient man. He never raised his voice or jumped at a sudden sound. Most of his expression came from his eyes. I can count on one hand the number of times he spoke sharply to me — and being spring-side is one of them.

He carefully lifted the gray trap door and rested it where the eaves met the floor. There, just beneath the dry flooring, was an awesome square, black space. A skin lay on the water like a worn piece of cheesecloth, letting little sparkles of reflection through its holes. I handed him a long pole tool with a net at the end like a net used for fishing, and he began to rake the scum. Then we paused, admired the water, and marveled that it was still there. Dad smiled slowly and almost gurgled his pleasure.

What we were admiring was the village water, and he owned it. It was a benign monopoly (which I think he rather relished) and a reminder of his beginnings.

Dad started out to be a businessman when he was just a boy, and he used the trains to make his money. Sheldon was a busy place back then when he boarded a daily run for St. Albans to sell newspapers and edibles. He raised rabbits by the hundreds and shipped them to the markets in New York and Boston. Not long before he died, I found a picture of him taken when he was nine or ten. He was standing in the farmyard, wearing overalls and dangling a briefcase from his hand, looking like a cross between a miniature farmer and a little businessman. He boarded away for high school and graduated at age sixteen, by which time he had already started his own insurance agency. While he was away at college, his mother acted in his behalf, collecting premiums and reminding neighbors when payments were overdue.

Dad was a grown man in his business prime when he acquired the spring, the Sheldon Waterworks. He could not have purchased the Waterworks as a financial investment because making money was his expertise and the yield from the village water supply was about as piddling as that from utility stops in a Monopoly game. I like to think he bought the Waterworks as a treasure of Sheldon's history. It was an ordinary spring by the time I saw it, but rare for a town that had once boasted its springs as the main attraction.

Sheldon, Sheldon Springs, and the Sheldons of compass directions such as North and East, produced extraordinary, healing mineral waters in the mid-nineteenth century, and the area had become the leading water resort in the country by 1870. The St. Francis Indians had called it "Medicine Springs" and given its water and sediments to Samuel de Champlain, Lake Champlain's European "discoverer," for his wounded soldiers. The white settlers took over the springs with the land, using the water like healing herbs. By chance, a wealthy New Yorker suffering from cancer of the tongue stopped in St. Albans on his way to Canada, drank a bottle of the liquid medicine, and completely regained his health within six weeks. That connection turned the native cooler into a commercial prescription, and the boom was on. Sheldon water was bottled and shipped across the country, an advertisement that turned the town into a bustling spa.

"We had every kind of water to cure what ailed ya," Gramma told me when she reminisced about her childhood in Sheldon's heyday. "There were a dozen hotels at one time, the water business was so good," she said.

Old postcards and photographs show the fashionable from New York and Philadelphia posed on the front verandas of huge hotels. The women are bustled and holding parasols. The men look like barbershop quartet conventioneers, dressed in stiff suits and straw hats.

Train tracks were laid to Sheldon when the spring waters with magical cures and cosmetic claims reached their commercial peak. The town boomed in the middle of rolling pasture land, fertile for grazing cows but also a balm for the city-weary. Visitors to the spa watched the hills of Vermont undulate in their rich green drapes under the summer light, and the Sheldon children watched the visitors. Gramma probably picked up a few pointers about being a lady, which she grew to be, but she mostly talked to me about the demise of the famous Sheldon spring business.

"Every summer we kids would go around to all the hotels and gawk," she said. "But the last summer was really something. The hotels began to collapse or burn, several in one season. We seemed to be running from one hotel to another so as not to miss the fireworks."

Sheldon came and went like resorts from Newport to Bar Harbor, perhaps because the springs ran dry or perhaps because all the city folk were healed. By the time Dad bought the village spring, after World War II, the eruptions of drinkable water had died down like the dwindling perk of a coffee pot pulled off the stove. I remember our relatives grumbling about the quality of the water and its scarcity in August.

My treks to the springhouse with Dad never really amounted to more than making sure it was still there. A need for repairs or an unusual murkiness would prompt him to say he would speak to Uncle Robert. "He'll know who should do it," he remarked as he checked the door. We both knew, however, that the job would be done by Uncle Robert after we left town.

Dad had that special relationship with Sheldon that small town natives earn from doing well "away." He had determined early that farm work was hard work physically and that brain power could surely equal a lifetime supply of gray mares. He had the brains. The oldest of five children and the only boy, he reckoned that the milking load would be his if he stayed around. Everyone from home encouraged him to go away. He earned his diploma from the University of Vermont at age twenty, and before he was thirty he had become Vermont's Commissioner of Banking and Insurance and the youngest trustee by decades of his alma mater. George Aiken, Vermont's governor at the time and a country boy himself, stood behind my father through the late 1930s and early 1940s while he challenged big institutions to follow honest economic practices. Dad made front-page news for months, I later learned while going through his papers after he died.

Of course, I also learned, from reading the yellowed newspaper clippings, what was happening to my parents' lives when I was born in 1940. While my father was being raked over the public coals for requiring audits in banks and in the university, surely my mother felt the private heat. That kind of pressure can turn normal domestic waters into a geyser.

Every place he went, Dad perked like his home town's bubbling springs, a good clean country water, bottled and shipped for what ails the city folk. He returned to Sheldon to fill his deepest needs with a thirst like the one that comes from haying all day in the July heat. He brought his college chums, his bride, his business friends to taste the best of country life — his father's food. Grampa cured hams with a maple syrup recipe that alchemists would envy and aged the kind of cheese that gave Vermont Cheddar its good name. He raised strawberries so big and red and juicy that people came from beyond the county line just to buy them. The maple sap he tapped and boiled to syrup lingers in my taste buds still — a shiny, sweet amber thread to the memory.

Dad returned to Sheldon in what must have been his time of deepest need: to ask his parents to parent his children. Now there's a thirst! Perhaps that is why the springhouse seems so important to me.

I went along with Grampa once to clean the spring. It was a few months before he died and early in the fall when time itself seems the most precious thing to enjoy. He called out a phrase like Frost's: "I'm going out to clean the pasture spring — you come, too."

Grampa was tall and skinny, straight and quick. He wore overalls every day, and when he worked in the burning sunlight he wore a broad-brimmed hat. Like a calf at the weaning stage, I followed him from the house to the barn and then across the road and off to the pasture. I wore overalls, too, and funny brown leather shoes. My hair was parted in the middle with a ponytail pulled off from each side of my head, and I thought I looked like a little calf with floppy ears.

Grampa chose a route through the pasture according to the cattle. He knew which field had bulls and which lay fallow. While I lingered to pick wildflowers, he waited for me at a fence, his hand and foot holding open an oval place in the barbed wire for me to crawl through. I stumbled behind, mounting each gray rock or boulder in our path. Down by the stream the pasture looked like a dried-up riverbed, more stones than grass. Grampa waited for me at the stream, holding out his brown arm beneath a rolled-up shirt sleeve. He must have spent more time waiting that morning than walking as we mounted the slope, my little legs lagging from fatigue. At the wood's edge he stood erect, like an oak that had survived the winds, waiting one last time for me to catch up.

We could see the springhouse through some hardwoods towering over a mossy forest floor. As we approached the house from its backside, we could see a bare spot on the roof where shingles had fallen off. Grampa grinned as he worked open the little door, crawled inside, then came back out immediately with a hammer and other tools.

"No need luggin' what you know you'll have to have only half the time," he told me as he set to do the job.

I hung around the clearing, impatient to go inside the house, while Grampa replaced the shingles. Just before we entered, he put his big brown hand on my little shoulder and "read the rules," an expression he used to keep discipline without hurting feelings. "The water's deep and it's bigger than the hole," he said. "It goes beyond the floor, Little Peanut, and if you fall in, it could catch you underneath. No monkeyshines 'cause I can't save you from this hole."

I stayed away from the edge, as Grampa said, while he cleaned off the scum. He worked until he was satisfied. I held the pail while he skimmed, and then he emptied it outside, leaving me alone beside the spring.

It was a moment of eternal trust. I was frightened but fascinated. By then my eyes had adjusted to the darkness. I could clearly see the black water and feel its infinity. Still moving from Grampa's cleaning, the water lapped against the floorboards, and it sounded as if it were saying, "Rest, thirst, and wash."

"Rest, thirst, and wash," I listened to the water's message.

That spring water was like a person's eye, the window to the soul, something that communicates without words. It is a memory, a way of life, a source of strength.

Dad eventually sold the Sheldon Waterworks, and people dug their own wells. Over the next few decades, the town shrank as the cities swelled, a kind of demographic evaporation.

Today the pastures are still filled with herds of cows, and young families are determined to see dairy farming through. The rocks and boulders have not moved from their ancient water bed, and the pastures still undulate under a Vermont summer light. The Sheldon waters are no longer bottled to sell for "what ails ya," but they linger just beneath the surface of the town's pastures like the water beneath the springhouse floor.

□ □ □ □

CHAPTER 3

Cousins

"We take care of our own," Grampa told us while he was milking. "If someone in our family is wanting, we take 'em in."

Anyone could see that was true. Grampa and Gramma had taken on my brother and me, and two of their daughters' families, who lived across the road, put up relatives from Connecticut in the summers. There were often a dozen cousins scampering around three kitchens, as many sheds and barns, and "all out-doors," and the adults never complained that we were underfoot. We were being raised according to a recipe that had not been tampered with for generations, the way delicious sourdough bread comes from a well-kept starter in the pantry. The secret to the recipe was that children worked or "helped out" right along with the grown-ups, and there was no waste of time or energy or table scraps.

"No waste with scarcity," Gramma proclaimed her farmhouse logic as she stacked dirty dishes that looked clean. "Make do with what's around you. God's given us an abundance, and you just use your little noggins to see what's here."

There was no abundance of store-bought toys or stuffed animals or even rubber balls. By "abundance," Gramma meant the matter of our daily lives and how we learned to use it.

Grampa's barn was our favorite place to be. He had a few cows that kept a steady heat, and in the wintertime the stacks of hay served as insulation. We swept and shoveled to keep it clean. When we finished with our chores of bottling milk and feeding pigs and chickens and one old mare, we pretended we were pirates jumping ship by swinging from the hayloft to the barn floor.

In the summertime we congregated around a small porch off Aunt Cynie's house. It had two posts holding up a tiny roof that sheltered a worn wooden floor nearly level with the ground. I bet we each crossed that porch in play a thousand times a summer. It was a sort of transfer station for freight as well as people, holding bushel baskets full of fruits and vegetables for "putting by" and laundry baskets of clothes and sheets to be hung out or folded. Adults often stood there like the baskets and made decisions about the children's play or chores.

Between my aunts' homes there were two large maple trees and a small yard where we romped all over our green Vermont summer carpet. At dusk we played kick-the-can or tag and caught lightning bugs in glass jars. We hung around the back gardens waving rhubarb stems like raving knights in armor, perfected cartwheels on the sloping lawn like circus acrobats, and begged for treats from aunts. The women were busy preserving foods to last through winter, and they invented delicacies from scraps to feed us.

"You ragamuffins stay on the porch," Aunt Cynie would warn us. "I'll scratch up something." We waited for her special treat: sliced homemade bread she buttered and sugared to a grainy glaze, and in the autumn she spooned warm applesauce on top.

Something seemed preordained about the arrangement of cousins by age and sex. One family had boys my brother's age, old enough to hunt and fish without adults, and the other family had girls for me, young enough to giggle constantly. We seemed to produce laughter as if it were a full-time job, whispering and teasing quietly until the noise erupted into an explosion of happiness. We giggled unmercifully at Sunday dinners, those feasts of homegrown food and treasured recipes, until one of us was told to leave the table.

Two cousins, sisters to each other and great gigglers, took me in as one of them. They were the "fast-rising yeast" our grandparents needed to raise me as a latecomer to their old-fashioned recipe. The older one was Lizzie, tall and skinny with cropped black curly hair, and the younger one was Mary, short and sturdy with blond braids. I was in between in age and size, with brown braids and a look of both of them. They showed me the ropes of country life, how to make up games, and what to do in school. I learned the oral history of our village from my cousins who had listened to the grown-ups gossip. They instructed me as we passed houses on our way to school or picked up empty bottles along the road. Lizzie was the main teacher, but Mary always added something.

"Mrs. Battles got a hip displacement," Lizzie pointed to a white clapboard house in need of paint.

"Her son's demented, too," Mary shouted.

"Sssh, we don't know for sure," Lizzie whispered. "Now, next door to Mrs. Battles lives a creamery worker, the man rocking on the front veranda. See!"

"He's Catholic, too," Mary said.

"Well, so are we," Lizzie had the final word.

They took me to the library, where we were not allowed to giggle. It was in someone's house, a little room with books and a window overlooking the pasture and the creek from the same perspective I had from my bedroom window.

My pet recollection about my favorite cousins involves that creek. It was canning season, and we had spent the forenoon snapping green beans. Our giggles and considerable begging to go wading in the creek brought the women together for a conference on the little porch. Gramma checked with Grampa about which pastures were wet or off-limits, and my cousins' mother, Aunt Cynie, packed a lunch.

"You do as Lizzie says," Aunt Cynie lectured us. "Don't dally too long, though. I begin to worry."

We took a paper bag filled with sandwiches and yellow cake with maple topping, a milk bottle filled with red Kool-Aid, a bar of soap and one towel, and headed off to the cool creek. We picked our way through fences and yellow ocher-colored grass and stopped to look for frogs in murky pools. Of course, we laughed with every leap. About what? No one remembers; but even now as grown women, when we recall the giggling times we start to laugh again.

When we entered the line of hardwoods along the creek, it felt as cool as a cave. Trees from both banks met above the water in a warp and woof of leaves and branches. Sunlight filtered through the weave; and mixed with rising moisture from the moving water, it looked like lemonade. The rushing water inside the lacy cave gave great booming laughs against the boulders, which echoed in a round. We could hear the wet and see the cool.

"I'll beatcha in, I bet," I hollered.

The creek had rocks of every kind. We sat on jagged rocks to strip off shoes and socks and slipped on mossy rocks to step on rounded stones. A creek is smaller than a river but bigger than a stream, a mid-size collector of stones and rocks and boulders where mountain water fills the crevices. Our little feet fit neatly into the ice-cold spots. The sensation recharged our giggles in an imitation of the water's laughter, and we withdrew to scurry down the bank. Lizzie found a quiet sandy place to wade, a lone pool protected by nature's dam from the rushing waters. We ran in and out of the cold water until Mary sat boldly in the middle of the creek and then suddenly scrambled out when I said I saw a leech. We all giggled while Mary splashed me for having teased her out of the cool pool, and after she had soaked me from head to foot, we picked our way across the creek by stepping on exposed rocks that looked like giant tortoises and speculated about what would happen if we could not return.

On another day, we once overstepped our childish boundaries when Lizzie was teaching me about wildflowers. She and Mary took me to the woods beyond the pasture behind their house. We crossed lumpy fields and a stream that barely trickled between great boulders, and then we crept along the inside of the woods but kept the field in sight. Suddenly, we stopped giggling and caught our breath.

"See the trillium, the trillium," my cousins sang.

There, right at the base of a huge tree where the trunk disappeared into its roots, were bunches of trillium, looking like a mass of stars scattered on the forest's floor. The little white sparkles in the dark woods danced before our eyes while we sang out their name.

"There's something even prettier, a great surprise," Lizzie told me. "But it's in deeper."

"And later in the season," Mary corrected her.

Later in the spring, my cousins took me for a walk to see the great surprise.

"Don't be long," their mother said. "I tend to worry."

We walked the same lumpy field, which was squishy from a wet season, and crossed the high stream. Then we entered the woods and passed the place where we had seen the trillium. We crouched and crept over fallen branches until we lost the fields from sight.

"It's gotta be here," Lizzie muttered. "It's that time of year."

"We gotta get back home, Lizzie," Mary scolded. "Mama will be awful mad if we get lost."

The forest was scary and we had gone too far, but I still felt secure. If we were lost and it was dark and cold, I thought we could just giggle to keep warm.

Liz finally found the great surprise peeking up between dried leaves and a rotten log. It was the most magnificent flower I have ever seen. There stood a lady's-slipper all puffed out in pink and white and its leaves spread about it like welcoming open arms. I leaned over to greet it.

"No, no, don't pick it," Lizzie grabbed my arm.

"It'll never grow again if we take it from its home," Mary explained.

I learned about delicacy and beauty as we stood in awe, an experience only rivaled in later years when I stood before a Renoir painting or a Monet.

We got home all right.

"No need to worry, Mama," my cousins said in unison. I felt lonely in that moment because Mary and Liz had a mother on the spot to worry about them. Perhaps that is why the day's experience of seeing a wild orchid in the deep, dark woods became so firmly rooted in my memory.

Sometimes we played inside games with scraps from the adults' work. The three of us made a pretend grocery store in their father's barn. We set wooden cartons on their sides for shelves and spent hours rearranging empty Quaker Oats boxes and tins of Spam, old bottles of vanilla and tins of baking powder. Other cousins would stop by to ask for something we did not display or say they could not pay their bills. On rainy days we made paper dolls and cut out clothes for them from some catalog, "Monkey" Wards' or Sears', or strung buttons into necklaces and bracelets.

When we went to St. Albans, called "The City" by village folk, we made up a game to amuse our silly selves while the grown-ups shopped. Liz, Mary, and I stuffed ourselves into the front seat of their father's car where it was parked facing the sidewalk and peered over the high dashboard at the pedestrians walking by. We had numbered ourselves off: "one" for Liz, "two" for me, and "three" for Mary. As people passed by, we numbered them as well. Number "one" was an old man who looked like he had not shaved for days and we tee-heed that he was Liz; the second passer-by, number "two," was a big woman with a funny, bright red hat and orange coat, so I took the heat for not knowing how to dress properly; and number "three" was a woman with two small children in a stroller, and she matched Mary's number.

"Ha, ha," Liz and I teased Mary. "You've got two brats to take care of."

"Ha, ha, yourselves," Mary reminded us that the babies would be numbers "one" and "two" when we started counting again. "You're the brats," Mary said, "and I'm the mother. I'm going to wheel you right past the candy store."

The game was one of chance and poking fun without harm and, as Gramma might remind us, it came from the richness of our imaginations and not some boxed amusement from the store.

The growing up by the old-fashioned recipe was just an overlap of work and play and cousins, "snappin' beans" and games of tag, pasture walks and school, and wading in the creek. It was a chain of older children teaching younger children, and it was made from scarcity.

Someone stopped by the barn one morning to ask about buying a pint of cream. Grampa was in the middle of showing a half dozen cousins and me how to harness a horse. He handed the bridle and bit to an older cousin, and the rest of us moved in closer to see how the mare would be outfitted. The customer muttered to Grampa that he did not see how Grampa could stand so many children around him all the time.

"Our grandchildren are underfoot, all right," Grampa said in a loud answer to the mutterer. "That's how we raise 'em." Then he winked at us kids and smiled as the cousin harnessing the mare slid the bit into her mouth and positioned the strap over the ears.

"Yup," he said proudly, "we've got a hands-on operation here."

□ □ □ □

CHAPTER 4

Country Medicine

Grampa set the tone for our entire extended family — whether we lived across the road from him or with him or away in cities, out of state. He had one strict piece of philosophy, and almost any one of us could state it without prompting.

"We might be poor," he would say, "but we eat well. That's all that really matters. Just good food. Helps you stay healthy and alive. Money doesn't do you any good if you're dead."

Grampa's home was the hospital of his time. There were glass canning jars of his "country medicine" on the shelves and smoked hanging carcasses in the cellar, and these came from the great vegetable garden between fields of wild spring greens and the barnyard of wandering potential edibles. We had two seasons of fruit harvesting to see us through the scurvy months, and protein provisions from those who set out to hunt and fish. There were cows that gave milk and chickens that laid eggs to bind a meal together in a nearly independent, self-contained environment. The flour was "boughten," the yeast and baking powder, too; but the sugar was homegrown — our kingdom was Vermont and we tapped our own.

At some point in March, depending on the time of the thaw, attention turned full force to gathering maple sap. School let out for two weeks or so, allowing nature to dictate vacation time, and we converted our playground energy into helping hands. Grampa hitched his mare to a flatbed, loaded it with buckets and grand-children, and set off across the pastures to the hardwoods that had been giving sweets for generations. There were maple trees down by the creek and several dozen peppered along the way. He bore a hole and sunk a spout a few feet up each trunk, then lodged a homemade hook above the source and gave us each a turn to hang a bucket underneath.

When the sap began to run, the excursion left off being fun. Grampa was a hustling person and expected us to be the same. Buckets needed to be fetched before they overflowed, sometimes twice a day, and taken to the sugaring house to fill the steaming vat. Inside the sugaring house it was warm, and a lantern hung over the vat in the windowless room, lighting the rising haze like the sun burning off a muggy day. A wood fire underneath the vat put out swirls of smoke through a homemade metal chimney like an answering message to the signals from sugaring houses up and down the valley. Grampa boiled the sap to syrup while the thaw outside continued, a time when folks worried about the river breaking up.

The Great Flood of 1927, when rivers spilled into towns and cities all over Vermont and washed out a thousand bridges and drowned people and cattle alike, was the source of the worry. Although that flood occurred in the fall after weeks of rain, rivers could rise just as quickly in the spring if the ice melted too fast. People had a palpable fear of the raging waters and tons of broken ice that could tear up our valley overnight. One of my uncles often reminded us about the spring when he had to walk the three miles to his graveyard shift at the paper pulp mill and back along the railroad tracks because its trestle bridge was the only way to cross the river and the roads were all washed out.

When I was four years old and living with my mother, she talked continuously that spring about how unsettling and dramatic the river was as it was breaking up. We were living across the road from Grampa and Gramma because my dad was serving in World

War II. He had settled my brother, my mother, her orphaned niece, and me in his hometown for the duration. My mother photographed the Missisquoi River as it was tearing past our town, and I have a stationery-size box filled with pictures of what fascinated her. They show the story of that year's quarrel between spring and winter: great white chunks of ice as big as sugaringhouse roofs piercing the banks and each other against a backdrop of the black river and dark gray sky. The photographs have come to represent the upheavals in my world at the time: one was global, World War II; the other was personal, the breakup of my nuclear family not long after my mother took the pictures.

When fresh snow fell during the sugaring season, we had ourselves a treat. My mother warmed the maple syrup to a special temperature and dripped it over a pan of snow to harden. Warm syrup still brings back my memory of that kitchen scene. The crystallized drippings looked like a pile of amber necklaces laid on white satin: the makings of an outfit for the "winter queen." We pulled maple syrup necklaces like taffy and laughed until it hurt.

When I lived with Gramma, she produced another treat from maple syrup all year long: a recipe she must have hammered out herself— "Rag Muffins" — twirled biscuits of leftover yeast dough wound like snails and baked in a pan of syrup and butter, then turned upside down to serve. They looked like a plate of anemones, with their dark centers and golden petals around the edges. "Rag Muffins" were my special medicine when things went wrong or I was feeling blue. Gramma would make a batch of muffins and leave them steaming on the table, all alone, just for me to snitch. It was a sweet filling for a sour soul, but it was more than that. It was a sign that Gramma knew when things were hard. Her knowing was the medicine.

□

Spring happened all at once. The rolling hills and pastures changed overnight like a faded comforter dipped in an emerald dye bath. "Vert-mont," the French words meaning "green mountains," contracted to Vermont, lives up to its name.

There may be no greener pastures in the world than the ones in a Vermont spring, lush alluvial soil supporting crops of grass spotlighted by a special angle from the sun. There is an urge to reach out and pet the hills, bright green faithful friends in healthy coats of lanolin.

"Come, Peanut," Gramma would call. "Here's the basket and a knife. Go down in McFitters' field and get a mess of cowslips."

She had several sets of encouraging remarks to send me on my way. I did not like to gather cowslips by myself; besides, I knew what the name meant.

"Now, don't bring home the ones with flowers," Gramma warned. "They'll be tough."

The yellow flowers, a kind of double buttercup, reached sunward on erect stems away from their humble leaves as if they, too, knew what their name meant. Cowslips are wild primroses — pretty, prim, and proper. They look like dandelions from afar, same height and same size flower, to someone who does not know her greens. The seasoned picker can tell, even from a great distance, which is which. One species shows in bunches like revivalists, and the other keeps a quiet distance from its neighbors like transcendentalists. The clue comes in knowing how they propagate — one by the windblown seed, the other underground.

It never mattered to me which variety I was sent to pick. Greens were a silly thing to eat, I thought. The grown-ups oohed and aahed over a mess of boiled and buttered greens and splashed homemade cider vinegar atop them as if it were holy water signaling reverence. I never ate the bitter vitamins in childhood, of course, but the tonic took hold years later. Now, each early spring I scurry around to dig and wash and steam some greens, fiddleheads or dandelions, and plant kale or rhubarb chard. My taste buds tingle from a message ringing in my ears.

"Eat your greens, little one," some grown-up voiced between mouthfuls of the stringy stuff. "It's just what the doctor ordered."

I never could see how the tonic worked, unless it served to raise spring fever instead of settle it. The adults were frenzied, rushing back and forth from barn to house to garden, lugging hoes and pushing carts. It was planting time, and the backyard activity looked like a Laurel and Hardy film at double speed. It was the time of year when children were not noticed and were too slow to be put to work.

"No rest for the wicked," Gramma would mutter as she hustled past me. In that season she was always moving, carrying something, and I seemed always still, sitting on a step, perhaps, practicing whistles through a blade of grass.

Spring became summer when the adults took seedlings from the windowsills and put them in the ground and we children began spending every waking moment out-of-doors. Grampa began to plant his one cash crop and, although the days were long in June, they were short for him. He had half an acre of strawberries to prepare and fertilize, and his frenzy set the pace as he enlisted his grown pregnant daughter to help him set out the plants. I was too young to work in the fields, so I sat at the kitchen table and looked out the window to watch my older cousins bend and pick when the strawberry harvest came on in July. They wore broad-brimmed straw hats as they worked slowly up or down a row. They looked like paper clips: one arm in the patch and the other curled under a basket handle, moving about their grandfather's business.

Grampa had a special room at the front of his barn (off limits to the field hands and lazy little spectators) where he worked and displayed his berries. The room had a wood-shuttered window, which he lifted when he was ready to sell. His strawberries were as red as Northern Spy apples after the frost and as big as early beets. He never let us watch him prepare the quart baskets, but we knew he had fussed over perfecting his product as much as a mother over her baby's baptismal dress. From the road one could see rows of vanilla-colored baskets filled with strawberries like sundaes and our grandfather standing erect behind them like a pharmacist behind a marble soda-fountain counter. People drove up from The City and across the county line to buy berries from him and waited in their cars or paced outside until he lifted the wooden shutter.

"Land sakes alive," Gramma would say, as she peered off the porch and wiped her hands on her apron. "Look who's here."

It would be someone she had "taken for dead" or a carload of primped ladies from a faraway town. During the war years, Gramma might remark that so-and-so had practically squandered their gas ration to make the trip or that Grampa's strawberries were "the only treat these days."

The strawberry spectacle, which I watched passively for weeks, culminated for me at our kitchen table with strawberries and milk and bread for supper (until the hives appeared), a better feast than the pink ice cream we hand-churned or the thick preserves we ate in the winter. My special bowl was deep, not too wide, and white with two blue stripes around the outside. Gramma filled it halfway with newly stirred milk and selected a few big berries to slice. I sat down beside the same window where I had watched Grampa's "paper clips" at work and took a piece of thick white homemade bread. There was no waiting for the cream to freeze or the preserves to jell. It was my strawberry supper, red and juicy, sweet and pure, right from Grampa's garden.

☐

One berry season bled into another until spring had shot through summer into fall. We had berry pies of every type with some rich red or purple filling underneath a flaky, rolling crust made with lard and butter. Throughout the summer Gramma's kitchen looked like a jewelry store with assorted jelly glasses and canning jars set on every shelf and table to cool. We had amethysts from currant jelly, rubies from raspberry juice, and diamond-studded black onyx from wild blackberries laced with sugar. When the berries disappeared and the kitchen work turned to canning beans or corn, we knew the sparkling family treasures were safely stored in the cellar vault for a rich winter.

Grampa had cleaned the cellar during his spring fever frenzy. There were shelves from floor to ceiling along every foot of the granite foundation and a set beneath the stairs and one in the cellarway, all forming a geometric maze. It seemed impossible in early summer that this cool medicine chest could be filled by fall. At the back, beyond the coal bin, he had sectioned off a special place for his hanging critters of ham and beef, spooky shadows when I fetched a jar or two in winter.

On my cellar trips to fetch some stored food item for Gramma, I scurried past the dark purple jars of blackberry jelly and remembered the season that had produced them and when my mother had been put away. My mother was more present for me there than anyplace because she was never in our conversations or in photographs or even in my dreams. Perhaps that is why forty years later, when I was gathering berries to "put by" some blood-red jelly of my own, I discovered that my mother had never really been absent from my life; she simply had been stored in the "basement of my life."

"You're my legs," Gramma would say as she directed me to go downstairs. "I want a quart of beans and a pint of pickled beets. Bring those up straightaway, and don't you fall."

I learned to diagnose what kind of occasion dinner would be by my cellar runs. A common meal — just family — would come from potatoes and some vegetables in a quart jar. Company meant smaller jars, a pint of pink-faced peaches or watermelon pickles. The tiny antique glasses, tucked on a little shelf by the cellarway where they could be seen when the door was ajar, were reserved for someone like Uncle Percy, an extra special visitor from away. The prize was rhubarb preserves: a pink agate shot with streaks of orange and golden brown. It had walnuts and orange peel, purchased delicacies too dear for everyday fare.

Summer was quick to go. It was green and lush with unwieldy weeds like thistle brush and fields of hay and corn. We played in the barn after milking time, chased the chickens about the yard, and teased the pigs from atop a wooden fence. We pulled carrots from the garden and roasted ears of corn by the riverbank on family outings. When we were not outside, we were on the back screened-in porch that overlooked the garden and the barnyard. There we churned butter in a wooden tub and chipped ice off the block before it was boxed. We turned ice cream after supper in the fading daylight and ate it as fireflies spattered the darkness. While we were shelling or snapping for canning, someone was always squeaking either the old cushioned metal couch on its rusty frame or the old dried-out wicker rocker. We sliced carrots into orange coins and opened pea pods to discover light green pearls. We snapped beans or patiently slivered them from end to end so the oval dots appeared like buttons on a silk blouse. We husked corn and scraped it clean, then matched it with shell beans, little red and white marbles, for succotash.

As we sat less and less on the porch — when the days shortened to make room for the cool nights — our space was taken up with the final harvest. Pumpkins and squash of every kind were piled in a green and yellow collage, and potatoes and onions were sorted into big and small baskets like several sets of gears, and cabbage heads sat in the shadows beside tumbled rutabagas like croquet balls. The harvest was a blanket on our summer bliss, a final notice that we had no more time to gain protection for the year ahead.

Apples began to intermingle with the garden stuff: Wolf-Rivers — great green balls — for baking, and McIntosh for applesauce. There were crisp Cortlands, yellow ones, and Northern Spies to spare. Some were from our grandparents' prize trees, planted with grandchildren in mind, but the bulk were brought in from Grand Isle.

Grand Isle, or Isle La Motte as the French named it, is a Vermont county made up of islands in Lake Champlain. Vermonters get right to the point and just call the territory "the Islands." The Islands lie in the middle of the great lake, which is surrounded by New York State, the Province of Quebec in Canada, and Vermont, and are connected to the mainland by bridges and ferries. The area is loaded with early American history and battle sites and with pre-European history. I do not know what the Native Americans called it, but I fancy something like "floating place." The Islands are flat and fertile and filled with apple orchards. They were not too far from our village, so in the fall we would load a car with big and little apple pickers, fill a basket with picnic food, and take off to Grand Isle for the day to pluck the round, red fruit from some grower's trees.

When I was nibbling Grand Isle apples, I did not know its history or that the source meant more to our family than just the best that nature had in mind. It was Grampa's heritage: Grand Isle or Isle la Motte. Grampa was one of a baker's dozen of children in a family of French blood with an English name who had rooted on Grand Isle. There is family lore that Grampa's "French" grandmother was really Indian. I sometimes think he was prejudiced in his liking for Grand Isle apples, reminders of where he came from.

Apples are about as much "Vermont" as maple syrup or Cheddar cheese. There is something in the soil that makes the red-skinned fruit pink inside instead of white. The applesauce from "Macs" picked after the first frost is as rosy as a January sunset. The red balls of fire kept a vigil year-round as a staple in our diet, and I equate their constant, healthy presence to the "floating place" where they were grown, which receives light from both the rising and the setting suns.

"This is my little apple blossom," Gramma would say with her arm about my shoulder as she nodded a hello to friends on Sunday mornings.

Gramma kept small tubs of apple butter — a dark brown, thick sweetener to spread on hot, homemade bread — in the cellarway. She cooked it down in an iron pot on the back of the wood stove as the fall days crisped our cheeks and we started wearing sweaters. She made pies all year long that kept the apple slices firm in a golden case and served them with chunks of Cheddar. As often as not, we started our day with cold apple pie and pan-fried pork chops or spicy sausage patties. Apples were our alpha and our omega, our breakfast and dinner, from fall through winter until "spring fever" time.

☐

Fall closed in quickly. The garden's bounty was put away just about the time the cellar was filled up. The shiny, multicolored glass canning jars reflected turning autumn leaves.

"I've got a mind to lay around a bit," Gramma would say about then. She was tired, anyone could see; but her words also signaled that the work was nearly done. There were a few more chores to do, the kind that trickled through the fall. We killed chickens — which means I watched. Water boiled on the wood stove while Grampa chased the feathery fowl below the porch. He was quick and lithe. One lanky arm caught the bird and the other swung to wring its neck. We had chicken stew with liquid gold gravy and dumplings, and we ate roasted birds that today's market cannot produce. It is a bygone art to raise a bird that sweetens and seasons without added salt or herbs.

The essence of Grampa's country medicine lies in a winter story. The cellar was packed with jars of his native prescriptions and the barn was warm from his few cows. It may have been a hundred feet from the porch steps to the barn door, just a dash in summer if I wanted to see the Ole Mama Cat that lived in the barn. In the winter it was another matter. One year, the snow piled in drifts nine feet high along the road. Grampa shoveled twice a day from the house to the barn and back again against the wind. The time came when the path seemed closed over, a solid block of snow and ice between the house and his work; yet Grampa still came and went from the barn to Gramma's kitchen. It was magic to me, just like the medicines for living he had prescribed.

One midmorning he showed me how he reached the barn. We bundled up in wool jackets and homemade mittens, tall galoshes and mufflers. He took my hand, and with his other arm he shouldered through the first snow bank by the door. I followed surely, and before I knew it we were in a tunnel: a dark purple way with scattered skylights. I was not scared, but the way was eerie. It was a long tunnel, and the sides were even, smooth, and tailored like white rabbit fur or a polar bear.

The barn was as warm as the kitchen. Grampa's strawberry room was closed off and the loft was shut. He had a few things to do, and I found the Ole Mama Cat to catch up on what she had been doing. It was a wonder to me that Grampa had carefully carved a tunnel from the house to the barn or in reverse. Which came first? I wondered. The barn or the house? That was Grampa's medicine: the interlocking between good food, hard work, and kin to teach.

Grampa died in his early sixties, from working too hard, his children said. Gramma died nearly thirty years afterward. It was the day we buried her beside Grampa, the man with the practical philosophy, that I saw the miracle. Gramma had gotten to be eighty-five, when she "had a mind to lay abed" forever, and she had never seen one of her descendants die. Here we had a large extended family, like some Old Testament description of God's people multiplying and then going on to plant and harvest the good earth's fruits, without any insurmountable physical problems. We had some misfortunes, yes; but no deaths or debilitating illnesses. I imagined Grampa smiling at his descendants and nodding in the affirmative at the miracle.

"Yup," he might have said, "good food sticks by you."

□ □ □ □

The Schoolhouse

In early September, right after the blackberry season explosion that removed my mother from my life, I started second grade at the country schoolhouse in the center of my grandparents' village. The schoolhouse was a magical place for me. It had big paned windows that warmed my soul, a janitor who parented me, one teacher who was clearly in charge, and a brilliant formula for learning.

Although I attended the schoolhouse for only that year, it impressed stability on my future. For the next six years of my elementary education, I moved six times and went to four different schools. These moves and changes were chaotic, but my second-grade experience was not. I needed the firm imprint of stability. The year before, I had been in the first grade and living with my parents in another state. My mother had walked me to and from school daily. There had been confusion in my classroom — four teachers in one year — and my mother, who was a teacher by profession, had sought to compensate by the consistent walks. We must have talked a lot — bonded, as they say. I missed her first and foremost when I started second grade and walked to the old-fashioned schoolhouse without her guiding hand.

I could see my new school from an upstairs window in my grandparents' farmhouse. It looked like a cathedral might have appeared to medieval people because it was built on the highest hill in the middle of the village. The two-story, bright yellow, buxom building had floor-to-ceiling windows on every side, upstairs and down, and was as much a part of our world in the 1940s as a Gothic church would have been for people in the 1300s. It was the centerpiece of our village where green mountains were pouring down through pastureland to the river like laying linens to dress a table. A railroad track etched along beside the river that carved through the valley and left town on its way to who-knows-where.

I walked to school with Mary and Liz. The schoolhouse was across the tracks and about six city blocks from home, but, of course, I felt it was miles away. Gramma gave me strict instructions about getting there.

"Now, Punkinhead, you do as your cousins do and as I say. Stay on this side of the road all through town until you've crossed the bridge. Then stop before you cross the tracks. Listen carefully for the train whistle. Take Liz's hand. Do it right 'cause I tend to worry."

Right after we crossed the tracks, we faced a natural outcropping, or a crag, and we really had to work at walking up the steep incline. The large embankment kept our schoolhouse from falling into the river the way a parapet might have protected a cathedral in the Middle Ages. The front yard was filled with grass patches, swings and teeter-totters, and a small merry-go-round — without the carousel figures — that we pushed ourselves. Like anxious horses at the starting gate, we dug deep holes with energetic feet underneath the iron toys until the playground was filled with craters like the moon.

There were giant shade trees in front of the school, under which we sat in warm weather to eat a sandwich, and a natural stockade of trees in back that surrounded a bare ball field. Fifty country children, everyone in grades one through eight, played in the protection of those old maple trees. On the Fourth of July, after a parade through town of horse-drawn carts and decorated wagons, the whole village gathered at the school yard to play funny games of competition: races with one leg tied to someone else's or both feet bound in a potato sack.

The schoolhouse was always glistening someplace, depending on the sun's position in the sky, so it looked like a gently twisting crystal ball. To run all around it, a favorite game, took half a minute or twice as long, depending on the runner's length of leg. There was magic in the course as if we were doing the exercises prescribed in some fairy tale—to get inside without going through a door.

There were two large entrances on opposite sides of the building, one for boys and one for girls. We hung our togs in a coatroom underneath the stairs and then met in the center hallway to resume some silly matter.

The wide hallway danced before my eyes in ripples and waves of gold where a glossy varnished hardwood floor stretched between two sets of stairs. The stairs' risers and banisters were polished in a matching sheen, and the stairways reached upward on either side of tall double-paned windows as if they were supporting arches of the edifice. The golden hallway was more than a place to pass through. Once a week we met there in convocation, and the stairway steps served as chairs. It was like meeting in an ancient marketplace to exchange and learn: The teachers were our artisans, and we were their apprentices. They were our Benvenuto Cellinis, great goldsmiths demonstrating crafts they had hammered out in isolation, and we stared in awe. One read an epic poem or a classic story aloud or coached a child or two to speak the parts. Another played her harmonica and taught us words to sing along. Certain river songs still trigger that harmonious pitch in my memory, and I am glad to have the company. The varnished golden floor, our stage, was large enough to hold eight children in a dancing square, learning calls and answering them with their feet. We laughed and clapped to keep the beat and watched them from our Acropolis seats.

When the golden hall emptied and children scattered to their classrooms, someone special was left to guard the place. He wet-mopped the yellow floorboards with a steady back-and-forth motion and kept his eyes on the older boys' behavior. Through the glass in the top of the classroom door we could see his head bop up and down and his suspenders stretch with each hurl and dip of the mopping up. This skinny, smiling older man was more than janitor: He was fatherlike to all the children and a real grandfather to six of us.

Grampa was the tallest person at the school, and he kept order for the four female teachers. He was quick and never missed the antics before they were fully formed. His eyes sparkled so behind wire-rimmed glasses that I might have thought he polished them at the same time he waxed the hardwood floors. There was very little hair on his balding head and none upon his face except his eyebrows.

"Give me a morning kiss," he had said at home as he grabbed me in a sweep. "I've got a special treat for you," he laughed as he lifted me up to his unshaven face and scratched my cheek. Every morning, after his barn work and before his shave, Grampa greeted me with a cheek-rub — the kind of daily tender strokes that older people use on children as if they were fine-sandpapering new wood. In school he treated me like the other children unless I was alone with him in the center hall.

"How's it goin', Peanut?" he would ask as he bent down to press his cheek against my forehead the way he did at home. "You're doin' fine," he answered for me. "Yup, I can tell."

My classroom, which Grampa cleaned regularly, was magnificent. There were floor-to-ceiling paned windows on two sides of the room. They were hardly ever shaded, so we could look outside, and the light was always welcome. The sun beat on our backs while we were students, and we faced it naturally when we played inside. There were overhead electric lights for cloudy days, but I do not remember that they were ever lit. Learning was a process, like photosynthesis, of older children helping younger children, and a teacher in the mix.

Our first- and second-grade teacher was principal of the school. Everything about her was brisk and orderly, even her thick brown hair wound behind her head. When we passed her house on our walks to school, we muttered disrespectful, childish sayings that we never repeated in the classroom. She taught our two classes and ran the school as if we were her orchestra and she were our conductor, measuring rhythm with a baton and indicating volume with her hands.

"This is Europe and this is Asia," she explained while she aimed a long pointer at the map.

She made us feel that what we were learning was as important as the work of those who first discovered what we took for granted. We moved from desk to desk in as serious an exploration as Mendel counting peas. Sometimes we were little Rembrandts when we finger-painted or Galileo and the Inquisitors when we argued over agates. When we were tracing letters in a practiced penmanship, we were scribes writing, and when we were memorizing, we were monks preserving texts. There were spelling bees, a long line of anxious letter-arrangers that dwindled to one winner. One wall was filled with maps and pictures. A large blue globe stood in the corner between a dark wall and a set of windows, and we spun it back and forth as if we were dictating night and day like prehistoric people who believed their rituals raised the sun and moon. We read words new to us in books that lay flat from years of opening, and we stared at colored illustrations as if they were cave paintings. We drew numbers, letters, and silly pictures on a blackboard that filled one wall, and we took turns erasing it.

Grampa tidied up our room while we were playing in the school yard or walking home. He washed the blackboard clean and swept the floors. His invigorated muscles, tuned from milking cows and lugging pails, worked to wax the yellow boards and wash the windows so our classroom shone like light itself.

When we descended from our school upon the parapet and stopped to listen for the train, someone always mentioned what was most upon our minds.

"I've got two pennies. My treat today," a cousin said.

We crossed the tracks to the grocery store nestled beside the bridge. The store had a candy counter underneath a curved glass top that was as colorful as a Tiffany shade lit up. Open boxes held big red balls that snapped our tongues like flames of fire and little balls of every color wrapped in a clear crinkly paper that set our teeth on edge. There were black licorice sticks and pink sticks of gum and cardboard sticks stuck into brown taffy or bright lollipops. Little yellow and orange triangles imitated corn, and green and pink wedges resembled miniature watermelon slices. There were fruity-tasting round pills of different colors wrapped into a roll, which we called "tiny rainbows," and flat shiny packages of bubble gum with picture cards. There were so many varieties of candy in the domed case, it seemed I would never taste every kind.

We unwrapped our tiny bits of glasslike candy and shared the sweet and sour treats as we crossed the bridge. There was one place where we always stopped, perhaps to finish off a trade or rest to savor a familiar taste. It was in the middle of the bridge and on the side with a paved walk. The railings were low, and the bridge's cover had long since gone. We peered over the side to watch the water wrap around the bed of rocks and leaned awhile to hear it splash. We were looking at the water below, the cool creek where we bathed in summer and the strong river that threatened in spring.

There is a curious recollection about our bridge stops to and fro, our only walks through town: We stood where others had stood before us, looking upstream but never down. We may have thought it was because Grampa's pasture bordered on the water up a ways, and therefore we were not far from home. We liked to see the water "coming" instead of "going," I guess, and we turned toward the source as instinctively as we had turned toward the light streaming warmly through the schoolhouse windows. The river was the greatest force we knew, cutting through our village and going who-knows-where, and the schoolhouse was our great diversion like a cathedral stretching upward with its dancing sparkling glass.

Those stops were a child's means of meditation, a kind of reflection, while the candy melted in our mouths and the water ran beneath us. The sweet meditative mood may stick in my memory because the river was like my life before and after second-grade — always moving — but for that moment, I was standing still, soaking up stability.

□ □ □ □

CHAPTER 6

Lillian Sings

The final Christmas with my mother had been an anxious one for me. Perhaps it was a preview of my parents' breakup and my mother's breakdown. On that Christmas Eve I whimpered on my bed in the darkness. My mother cracked the door ajar and came in with the hallway light as if she were an angel. She sat beside me, leaned against the headboard, cupped my head in her long arm, and began to sing a Christmas carol.

" 'It came upon a midnight clear,' " her voice slid gracefully up the scales. " 'That glorious night of old,' " she continued, and transported my tearful soul to the darkness long ago where stars splashed the sky like glittering gold. She knew all the verses by heart and sang so softly and reassuringly that my anxieties fell into the very darkness that had threatened me before.

My mother must have sung to me many times, but I only remember that Christmas carol. It may be because it was her last lullaby or because of the poignant season or because my grandmother, who sang like a bird before the break of day, picked up where my mother had left off.

Gramma, known locally as Lillian, was a country lady, as genteel and pretty as the city folk but specially seasoned from forty years of tending farmhouse-living with her own hands and spirit. When I put my arms around her, my head nestled between her waist and breasts where her cool, cotton dress closed in a line of buttons. She wrapped her warm, fleshy arms back around me as surely as lilacs blossom in May, and she smelled as good. She was soft to touch, just wide enough, and as erect as a staked peony in full bloom. Her thick, white hair was wound atop her head in knobby speckled strands of gray and white and yellow in an upsweep to a bun. In the intimacy of dressing, Gramma let me brush her hair, which spread across her back and down to where my hands met when I hugged her.

"I made donuts, Lazy Head," Gramma chirped some mornings as she continued in a kitchen rhythm. "They're behind the stove, underneath the towel, keepin' warm for you. Right there."

I had heard her making donuts hours before and singing, "Jesus calls us." Sometimes she measured out the next line with a hum, but more often she bellowed out "o'er the tumult" in lower notes as if it were a perfect echo or answer to the call. My bedroom was just above the kitchen, and Gramma's songs alerted me to a new day like an alarm clock that never failed.

Singing was so much a part of Gramma's biological makeup that I imagine she had as strong an urge to learn to sing as she did to walk. She just had it in her and needed to draw lines around her space in a clear voice. This handsome country lady sang when she cooked or cleaned and when she hung out laundry. In the sewing room off the kitchen, her voice whirled in tune with the foot-pedaled Singer. I never knew whether the machine or Gramma set the speed as the music stopped and started and the verses gathered around the making of a new frock. There was no interruption or embarrassment when folks intruded because she kept on singing as if that were her work. She "la-dee-dahed" a tune on errands to the barn or garden so one heard her coming like a cat collared with a bell.

Gramma was as much a product of our Vermont village as cows and maple syrup. I understood that best when we walked downstreet together.

"Lillian," a matron called from across the road. "We'll need your hands to put on the grange supper."

"Pot pie?" Gramma queried, keeping on her stride as if she knew the answer.

A dozen "Lillian-like" ladies made chicken pot pies, each as different as their cook's name, and served the village on some Saturday night. The grange hall, as big as a barn, where they held their benefit, was across the road from our house. Tables stretched from one end of the great open space to the other, and the ladies bustled all day to fill them with steaming vegetables, homemade pickles, raised rolls, and farm butter. I watched the preparations and ran to fetch some forgotten knife or masher from Gramma's kitchen. The ladies were all singers, so some tune from church was always erupting at one end of the hall and being finished across the way. When we lined up at suppertime (little boys in pressed shirts and little girls in starched dresses), the music came from sizzling hot pot pies. Each lady had her special recipe: home-raised fowl stewed until tender, some with vegetables but most without, and covered with biscuits or crust. We swarmed to sit by a favorite pie or to try a recommended one and laid bets about dessert. They finished off the benefit with big scoops of homemade ice cream and wedges of chiffon or fruit pie. Sometimes we ate two desserts, staggered home from overeating, and immediately put our sleepy heads to bed.

The special feast had been honed to perfection from generations of practicing tradition. Lillian came from the main line of stock in town and intended to see it through. People said she was a beauty when she was young and picked her man, a strapping handsome farmhand from the next county, and she aged like the maple trees her husband tapped for syrup — most brilliant in the fall. There was something sociological about Gramma's background that when combined, the way genetics are based on mathematics, made her a pure Vermont woman. She was French-Canadian (those high-bred people who moved south along the waterways), turned from a Catholic heritage to Protestant, and sometimes scornful toward her origins. She taught me how to kneel and pray at night, how to read by reading to me aloud, and how to pass a needle with fine thread. The heritage passed on most surely, like stories by the campfire, in her song.

" 'Rock of ages,' " she sang out, " 'cleft for me. Let me hide myself in thee.' "

It was a common church hymn to use when she was kneading bread, with a slow sure movement back and forth to keep the rolling dough in a turn upon itself. She knew all the words and sang every verse with the same confidence she had in baking bread. And then she hummed the tune with satisfaction as she laid the white sticky ball in a large light blue bowl to rise, covered it with a striped linen towel, and began another job.

☐

Gramma loved her church, and she took me every Sunday. We were an uncommon couple (an unwitting preview of the years to come), a stately country lady and her little girl. She wore some simple pastel dress and a small straw hat, and I was decked out in something that came off her Singer — a cotton dress with a large bow in back beneath my braids. Children who sit a full hour or more in church cannot remember what was said or prayed, and I have forgotten, too; but the singing is another matter. There was a rushing in the songs: anxious matrons pouring out in unison what each rehearsed alone at home while baking bread or cleaning up.

Tunes, buried melodies I have not heard for thirty years, come back to me when I am fussing with domestic things. Then I see the inside of Gramma's church again in my mind.

The church had light-colored walls with tall, arched, stained-glass windows and a deep red carpet that ran down the aisle between two sets of wooden pews. The only furnishings up front were an organ, a wall board to hold that Sunday's hymnal numbers, and one chair for the minister. Pipes rose behind the organist, who faced the congregation. She was more important than the minister because she came from town while he was from "away," sandwiching in our little church on a big circuit.

The organ was the heart of worship and, being of an earlier vintage, it was pumped by hand. Children took turns pressing the bellows to keep the important instrument alive, and I had my turn. It was as much an honor for little Methodists to pump the organ as being an acolyte in a sacramental service or a robed choir boy in a cathedral. Gramma insisted I take my turn to pump the organ, although I was embarrassed and reluctant, and she coaxed me softly by whispering encouraging words into my ear. The congregation could not sing until I arrived up front, and that pressure made me trip where the carpet was tacked to the floor. The organist whispered instructions as I looked at the tapestry-covered bellows, and suddenly I began. Pressing down, then lifting up, I heard the hiss but not the music. I panicked, as if I were breathing to resuscitate a victim who does not respond, and moved the handle in a frenzy up and down.

"It'll be too loud," the organist instructed, "if you pump so hard." I learned to gauge the volume needed by standing between the organ and the people and creating a rhythm of my own to pump the bellows rather than following the beat of the music. Pumping bellows was a mystery to me. How could it not be related to the timing of the organ music? It is like the great mystery of hearing someone's voice and words (or song) in my inner ear long after they are gone.

Gramma had a way of orchestrating matters as she saw fit. Grampa did not go to church too much, begging off for farm work or an hour to rest, but she reined him in when it was important. On Christmas Eve he played Santa Claus without the red suit in the basement of the church, where it seemed the whole village had gathered. The tree, some evergreen found among the maples, had real candles on the tips of branches and strings of popcorn wound around it. Grampa stood beside the tree and called each child to receive a small wrapped package for opening on Christmas Day.

For some, it was the only gift that year. Then we sang every carol in the book.

☐

The first year I lived with my grandparents, just before the Christmas feast, I sat on the floor at home making paper chains to string around our tree. It was tidy work: cutting strips of red and green and yellow papers to wind around each other and then pasting the circles together. I may have hummed a Christmas carol or something we had sung in church, imitating Gramma in the kitchen or around the yard. It had been a quiet fall because things had been hard on Grampa. Like a child told to sit still a bit, he had been sent to bed by the doctor. I did not know what was wrong, but it did not change the happy times. Gramma set a box of dress-up clothes, old shoes, and frocks with a few hats thrown in, at the end of their bed. I went upstairs every day and often brought a cousin with me to play make-believe for Grampa. We were little Lillians or farmers, trouncing back and forth with cotton skirts dragging behind clodhopper shoes, or in overalls without a shirt, and we acted out the parts we thought we knew.

"La-dee-dah," my cousin Mary shouted as she opened up a parasol to signal that she was a lady. "I'm Gramma, off to church and back by noon."

We laughed. And Grampa laughed, half sitting up in bed and leaning against the tall bird's-eye maple headboard. His thin shoulder blades poked up beneath his nightshirt, and his eyes sparkled behind his wire-framed glasses.

"I'm the farmer," I announced, dressed in overalls with a scarf around my neck and a straw hat to shade my eyes. "And I'll be home, Lillian, when you come back from town."

We pretended a skit for every event our little lives had seen, and we danced without music as we had seen actors pantomime in the silent movies at the grange hall. Grampa may have known, and we may have sensed, that our homegrown entertainment was the best medicine for his last days.

It was while I was sitting on the floor between the kitchen and the parlor and making the paper Christmas chain that I heard Grampa sing. It was late afternoon when day passes into evening. He was upstairs in the bedroom and Gramma was in the kitchen.

I heard him through the floor register but did not think it was important. Then he sang out again.

"Lillian," he cried. "Lillian." He sounded like the organ winding down when the bellows stop pumping air.

"Grampa wants ya," I said softly. "I heard him cry."

Gramma dropped her kitchen tool and rushed past me with a try at wiping hands on her apron. He was gone, of course, by the time she got upstairs, and they buried him before winter froze the ground.

It took growing up and raising a family of my own before I understood that Grampa was the pivot in the wheel of my extended family. When he died, a way of life went with him. No more farming or provisions from the sweat of our brows or taking care of what Gramma called "the all outdoors." Grampa had either shepherded most of the projects at home and in the village or shown others what to do. I recognized what we all missed in Grampa when I married someone who had those traits.

Even my father, when he was an old man near the end himself, spoke of Grampa as if he had just died and the grief were fresh. Dad leaned upon his cane and turned to look straight at me.

"He died thirty-five years ago, but I still miss him," he said as tears closed over his eyes. "I'll miss him until the day I die."

I knew what Dad meant, not from missing Grampa so much myself but from having tried to play his part. When Grampa died, Gramma and I were left alone to fill each other's empty spaces like water searching for a place to go. We slept together in their bed and later in several other beds as we moved from place to place, keeping warm by lying back to back. She closed up the farm, like shuttering up a summer kitchen in October, and we left country life behind to live in cities. Gramma made the best of our new life, which I think she neither understood nor liked. She brought along a few things to keep in touch with home: photographs and crochet patches, worn linen tablecloths with faded stripes along their borders, and cotton dresses — some for her and some for me. She unpacked her Singer and she sang her songs.

"Are ye able, said the Master," her alto voice sang steadily as she began a daily chore. And then she rang out the great refrain in one long, lung-filled bellow of "Lord, we are able."

She kept her voice in tune and her maternal task of raising me going until some spirit broke and she just gave in and went back home. My father had moved us to Montpelier, Vermont's capital city, and then halfway across the country to Kansas City, a mecca of urbanity to Gramma, and that is when she became dispirited. The pace and noise and style of living drove away my country lady. She may just have been a rural-rooted woman or she may have felt Grampa was more present in her hometown than where we lived, so she moved back to their little shuttered farm-house.

I missed her immeasurably. I had lost another mother and she had left a child, which was against her homegrown rules. Leaving me must have added to Gramma's grief. However, I imagine she kept on singing to lift her spirits. I know she hummed because I saw her rocking in a chair beside a window and keeping rhythm with a soft tune not long before she died.

Gramma died twenty-five years after she stopped mothering me. It was in the fall when Vermont's hills blaze in the same colors as an open fire and sear beauty in our memories for the long winter ahead. After her burial and one last sweeping glance at the familiar valley, which looked to me, at age thirty-four, like my pile of colored paper strips Grampa never saw on the Christmas tree, we walked back to my aunt's house to feast and claim our shares of Gramma's legacy. Her whole estate rested in a small cardboard box. There was a large family Bible, a stack of old photographs, crochet patches, and some costume jewelry. It seemed a paucity of things for such a large family, but it filled our hungry souls the way five fish and two loaves of bread fed five thousand.

But she left me something special, and I hear it whenever the need occurs. A tune wafts in unexpectedly when I am kneading bread or hanging laundry on the line. The opening phrase of an old hymn bursts from my mouth.

" 'Are ye able,' " I suddenly sing out.

" 'To believe that spirit triumphs,' " I can hear Gramma picking up the next line. The verse poses a great question about faith, but I am thinking about what Gramma gave me.

"Lillian," I answer, "thank you for my voice."

CHAPTER 7

□ □ □ □

Grampa and the Ole Mama Cat

It was only four months after I came to live with my grandparents that Grampa died. However, I remember being their last and only child that fall as if it were my total childhood. They were my spiritual parents, and Grampa's barn was my spiritual home.

"Where's the Ole Mama Cat?" I asked Grampa while he was milking. I was just a little jumper, no taller than the cow's leg I was standing behind.

"Now, Peanut, move away," Grampa answered the emergency rather than my question. "The ole girl'll kick you likely as not. She's testy today." He kept at the rhythm of pulling teats as if he were counting out the steps of a slow fox-trot. Grampa shot a stream of warm milk into a saucer and handed me the dish without missing a beat. "Here. The cat's about someplace. Take this to the packing room and just call, 'Kitty.' She'll come."

The packing room was Grampa's barn office converted from an old horse stall. The hinged window on the outside wall let a stream of sunshine into the darkness like the gold highlights in a Rembrandt painting. The little room's name came from its important function during strawberry season when Grampa sorted the prime red specimens into quart baskets and then crates, a task he enjoyed far more than paperwork.

The Ole Mama Cat assumed the room was hers all the time — a sort of total living space where she slept and bathed and birthed. She was a true farm cat, an undomesticated barn mouser, who appeared one day without invitation and simply stayed forever, the way a relative who hits hard times comes home. I felt like the Ole Mama Cat, except I was at the beginning of my stay and she was near the end. She was my best friend on the farm, partly because I liked her name and partly because she lived where Grampa worked.

I followed Grampa everywhere he went because he was my security and protector. He was easy with children, not abusive but strict, and a believer that experience was the best teacher. My trust in him came instantly. The moment I stepped out of my dad's black Ford to take up residence with my grandparents, Grampa reached his long, sunburned arm out to clasp my little hand and beckoned me to follow him.

"Come on, Sweet Pea," he said in his soft deep voice. "We've got kittens in the barn. The Ole Mama Cat had another litter yesterday."

My new life began in Grampa's barn as surely as if I had been a kitten in that litter. I loved the barn immediately. It smelled sweet and sour from milk and hay, and it had a silky feeling from moisture in the air. The front doors opened wide enough for a team of horses to be led through abreast. If the back doors were opened at the same time, to let the cows go out to pasture, the first floor looked like a cathedral lit up for services. The granite foundation was six feet deep at the back where the ground dipped, and steam rose off the heated rock and dung. Just beyond the hazy exit was a salt lick and troughs and then an interlace of fences where the cows waited to be led through. The pastures were filled with rocks and scrubby grass and pockmarks like honey comb from the small herd's hooves, and they dipped down to the maple trees that lined the river. The fields were a mixture of a yellow ocher color and vibrant green and, depending on the season, one always dominated the other.

That first afternoon, Grampa introduced me to the Ole Mama Cat who was nursing two kittens in a box of rags in the packing room. She was a short-hair calico, her rich brown fur streaked with orange and yellow veins like an agate or Italian marble. The cat smiled at me. People say cats cannot do that nor do they care to, but this cat did. Perhaps she had gained content- ment with age or she understood I needed friendliness. The old cat's belly sagged from two dozen pregnancies and constant nurs- ing. She had produced more than one hundred kittens in fifteen years, giving rise to lots of speculation. Each litter, different in color and length of hair from the previous one, brought out someone's recollection about the neighbors' toms. My cousins caught me up on the kittens I had missed.

"We've had orange ones. They're always boys," the report began. "And lots of calicoes. They're girls. There've been gray and black ones, and once we had an albino."

"Not albino," another cousin corrected. "T'was pure white, though. Only color on the thing was its pink-rimmed eyes."

The Ole Mama Cat's first litters were so large, eight or ten, that the stories sounded as if she were The Old Woman Who Lived in a Shoe, but by the time I sat beside the rag-filled box, her brood had dwindled to only two, a black one and a calico. I named the kittens and carried on a conversation with them by speaking both parts.

"Oh, Kitty, you're my friend," I whispered to one cupped in my elbow.

"Will you stay?" Kitty asked.

"I live here," I almost purred. "You'll see me every day."

☐

Grampa was like a guardian angel, leading cows and grand- children through a maze I count as heaven in my memories. He decided when the hayloft was fit for jumping and who could milk the cows or feed the pigs and when the fields were right for picking flowers. If we should venture into the back pastures to forage for bouquets, Grampa always stood at the barn's back foundation to see us off. We picked wild asters, goldenrod, and burst milkweed, and we kept our eyes on Grampa moving in and out of the mist behind the barn.

When we hitched the final gate and told Grampa we were safely home, we could see he had lingered with the pitchfork as a prop so we would think he had work to do and not worry on his mind. Grampa was tall and thin, and he stood as erect as the tool he held. He had a semicircle of short gray hair around his bald head, and his high cheekbones bumped his glasses when he smiled. He wore buckled overalls and dirty boots and often had an apple or half a donut in one hand. Grampa did every kind of work around the farm, including hauling laundry and hanging it on the line. He walked with long strides and leapt stairs by skipping steps.

"Lordy, he's always on the run," Gramma complained.

When Grampa did odd jobs beyond his barn, he either took me with him or he was working where I went. He was sexton at church and fix-it man at the grange hall, caretaker at the cemetery, and janitor at school. The lanky man's paths and mine crisscrossed about the village the way a burlap grain sack is woven, loose but sure.

In between Grampa's chores I checked on the Ole Mama Cat and her kittens. I often took tidbits from the kitchen to my new friend, but that practice of generosity did not start until Gramma had bent the farmhouse rules.

"The farmhouse rules," Gramma explained when I arrived to live with her, "include several about cats. First, we don't have any in the house. They're an underfoot liability. Secondly, the only kind we have are barn cats, and they're wild and belong outside." Gramma stopped talking and pressed two fingers to her head as if they would help her memory.

"Oh dear, I forgot the number of the next rule," she said. Then she smiled when she saw me holding up three fingers. "Well,

Peanut, I see you're listening. The last thing about cats is we don't feed them. They feed themselves. That's what they're for."

I often stood at the kitchen door, holding the Ole Mama Cat under her sagging belly until Gramma agreed to compromise.

"Oh, okay, I'll let you do something I never let the others do," Gramma said as she passed me a small dish of cheese crumbs through the doorway. "I can see you need the friend."

When I came home from school for lunch, I hurried through a meal of bread and gravy or a scrambled egg while Gramma was busy skimming butter fat on the back porch or doing laundry with a washboard and a wringer. I saved something for the Ole Mama Cat and skipped past Gramma to the barnyard. The Mama Cat was stretched out beside the granite foundation, watching her kittens play in the midday sunlight. They rolled together like sticky balls to make a snowman and danced on their hind legs as if they were fencers flashing swords. I told the Ole Mama Cat about school while she ate the morsel, and then I let the kittens finish fighting on my lap and lick my fingers clean of gravy. Their little faces looked like triangles with fans of shiny needles, and their purrs and cries sounded like a sewing machine in need of oil. They bit my arms until the Ole Mama Cat finished eating and moved them on to a new place to play.

Then I walked back to school. Grampa will be there, I thought as I caught up with my cousins. He seemed always to be right where I needed him to be. At school he was watchful and protective, but he never interfered unless the older boys were rowdy. He treated children the way the Ole Mama Cat raised her kittens: He kept a presence but extended a corrective hand, or paw, only when necessary.

"So, how was school today?" Grampa asked when I came home in the afternoon as if we had not seen each other all day. "Make new friends? Good." He shook his head up and down before I could answer yes or no. "Come along and tell me all about it," Grampa waved me to the barn. I had lots to talk about because it was approaching Halloween and we children were quite excited.

"I've got more work to do while it's still daylight," Grampa informed me while he swept up a pile of sawdust and I straightened out the rag box in the packing room. "Grab a rake, Peanut, and we'll trudge on up to the cemetery for a lick and a promise."

"A lick and a promise" was a household phrase that meant a quick once-over of dusting before last-minute company arrived and a promise to be more thorough later, so I knew the work would not be taxing. I followed Grampa down the road like a calf tripping off to pasture. We both wore overalls and brown shoes as thick as hooves and wide-brimmed hats to shade the autumn sun. I dragged the rake along the dirt roadside path to make swirls behind me and pretended I was a wagon pulling harrow and Grampa was my horse. We turned onto a dirt road that ran through huge orange-colored maple trees to a small old cemetery and then to a bigger one that Grampa clipped and mowed.

While Grampa worked, I pictured the cemetery as a theatre with three hundred seats. The rows of granite stones on the steep hillside were the audience looking at a stage of Vermont beauty. There was a backdrop of dark blue mountains in the distance, and then in closer relief were green hills beyond the village, and right before our eyes were bright orange, red and yellow trees filling the valley. The landscape was the performance: dancing Indians around a fire as the clouds slowly dipped and raised across the dark mountains and the setting sun. Behind the top row of tombstones was a dark green curtain of fir trees where I knew blackberry bushes grew. Spotty shots of the dusk light pierced through the thick forest like ushers' flashlights' beams through hanging green velvet, waving ticket holders to their seats.

One stream of light beamed on Grampa as he bent to edge a stone, to tear away the moss, and then to clip the other side. He laid squares of sod on a freshly filled grave and stomped it down as if he were playing hopscotch. I made piles of leaves beside a fence of maple trees and jumped each one as if I were playing leap frog.

"Come here, Punkinhead," Grampa beckoned. "I need your hands to mulch a bush."

"Will anyone come out?" I asked fearfully because the project was beside a gravestone.

"No, you silly goose. The dead are dead. When they're gone, they're gone. I put no stock in ghost stories and don't you either."

"But where do they go, Grampa?" I wondered aloud as I looked at the valley that had stopped dancing because the sun was going down.

"I suppose to heaven, Little One. That's what your Gramma believes. She's teaching you to pray, isn't she?" Grampa answered with a question and looked straight across the stone into my eyes to be sure the profound query had taken. "Well, yes, you just learn from her. She's a mighty smart woman." Grampa patted leaves around the bush's roots for a few moments and then said as he stood up, "And she'll be madder than a wet hen if we don't get moving. It's almost dark."

Grampa and I walked home while chomping on apples he had stored in his bib, and then we stopped for a moment to enjoy a favorite contest.

"I'll betcha can't hit that fence across the road," he challenged me as he pulled his throwing arm behind his head to pitch the core.

We laughed as two white spools spun high like meteorites and hit the dark horizon with a thud among the leaves. Grampa held my sticky hand on our last leg home to the little farmhouse underneath two giant maple trees. In the only lit window we could see Gramma working alone, and, being late October, the house looked the part of a pumpkin with just one eye carved out. I followed Grampa into the barn where he had milking chores to do, and I paid that day's final visit to the Ole Mama Cat.

"Ya wanna come inside? I betcha do. Poor thing. Ya'll be cold tonight," I chattered on while I tried to tuck her kittens into the rag box as if they were my dolls. I remembered what I had heard the grown-ups say about their future home.

"No one will take them," Gramma exclaimed. "We've given away more kittens than we've got friends. Land 'o Goshen, they breed like rabbits." Gramma was always getting rid of kittens just in time for the Ole Mama Cat to give her more. Then she muttered as an aside, "Maybe the river again."

That fall the kittens grew to be early adolescents with legs too long for their skinny bodies, and they were cocky toward their mother who had left off nursing them. The Ole Mama Cat took to lying in her rag box and letting me sing and stroke her into sleep. She still bathed herself, although her fur coat was thin and her joints were stiff. She lay against the cardboard box to lick the inside of a leg or her hairless stomach. The Ole Mama Cat's yellow eyes seemed to trust me more as the weeks went by, and I thought she expected me to find families for her pair. I asked every child at school I dared to speak to and quickly learned kittens were nothing special beyond their usefulness. All the farms were overstocked.

☐

It was around Thanksgiving when Grampa stopped milking cows and doing odd jobs. The doctor prescribed bed rest for Grampa, who muttered that it was not so much a punishment for him to stay still as it was a "downright sin."

"I've never laid abed my whole darned life," he swore as strongly as I ever heard him speak. "Jiminy Cricket, this is for lazy city folk. This is just the foulest thing I ever did."

He half sat up in bed and leaned against the headboard the way the Ole Mama Cat lay against her box. My visits with both the cat and Grampa kept me going to and from the barn. The Ole Mama Cat listened to my tales about looking for homes, and Grampa asked me questions about school.

"How's it goin'?" He would perk up when I came into his room. "I don't know how you get along at school without me there. The big boys — are they behaving?"

Grampa went downhill quickly and died between Thanksgiving and Christmas. The day they buried him, my cousins Mary and Liz and I stayed home to tend their newborn sister. We giggled hysterically from grief; we had no precedent for Grampa's dying and no understanding of what burying could mean. I just imagined Grampa lying down on the brown patch to be buried and then finishing the cemetery business the way he always did after folks had gone home. There was no snow upon the ground so he could still play hopscotch on the little squares of sod.

Before ice covered up the river, an older cousin made a trip down there with a worn grain sack filled with rocks. I knew he had been sent to drown the grown kittens, but I did not count on the shock that went with that burial. It hit me when I put on my coat in Gramma's kitchen and snuck a piece of chicken dumpling into the pocket.

"Where're you going in this cold?" Gramma asked.

"To the barn," I answered casually to disguise the fact that I had stolen food.

"No one's there, Muffin. You know that. And it's plum cleaned out of animals."

"But I'm going to see the Ole Mama Cat," I pleaded. "She must miss her kittens."

"Oh, dear," Gramma explained as she reached to stroke my hair. "She's gone, too. The Ole Mama Cat would have more kittens, and I can't bear to do this again. Besides, we'll be cleaning up the farm, Peanut, and who'd take care of the poor thing?"

I never asked where my cousin dropped the sack, but I guessed it was over the bridge I crossed to go to school. I looked there for an empty gunnysack caught between chunks of ice in winter and wondered if the rocks I saw in spring were some that might have broken through the bag. I had a fantasy for the Ole Mama Cat that was like the one I had about Grampa stomping in the cemetery. I imagined that the sack had torn and the cats had surfaced from the river to survive.

I knew Grampa and the Ole Mama Cat, forces that had given me security and trust, were really gone, but I never buried them. I kept them living in my imagination—good company for crossing bridges, particularly when I cross alone.

II.

Motherless and on the Move

A Time to Weep, A Time to Dance

□ □ □ □

CHAPTER 8

Laughter as a Mirror

Laughter was a great part of my growing up. There were jokes and pranks, good storytellers and able listeners, and laughs about real life. Occasionally, laughter was a mirror image of some misfortune or a grief.

The day that Grampa was buried, Liz, Mary, and I laughed so hard we cried. We were too young to attend the funeral, so we stayed home and took care of their baby sister. We were ashamed of our uncontrolled laughter, although no one else ever knew about it; and we speculated about whether Grampa could see us after he was dead and, if so, what he would have said.

"Don't worry, little ones," Grampa might have consoled us. "I understand why you're laughing instead of crying. Good steady laughter brings the tears up and fleshes out the situation. It won't bring me back but it will do you good."

Our laughter on Grampa's burial day, if measured by its potential to bring forth water through the eyes, would have been enough to resurrect the man. We chortled over diapering the baby and choked on something funny about wiping dishes, and each agreed to stop laughing if the others would. It was impossible, of course. Mary paraded through the kitchen with the baby's bonnet on her head and its straps tied beneath her nose; Liz tried to say "stop" while snorting, and I rolled across the floor in uncontrolled hilarity. We were downright beside ourselves.

Perhaps we knew that not only was Grampa gone but soon I would be gone, too. Not dead, but moved away. I finished second grade at the country schoolhouse and lived with Gramma for the rest of the year, but by the next fall Gramma and I had moved to Montpelier, the capital city of Vermont, too far away in 1948 to keep in touch by visiting.

Mary, giggling, would have corrected my word "visiting." "We don't visit, you silly goose. Grown-ups visit."

"And we giggle at what they say," Liz would have reminded us.

Liz was right. Except I stopped giggling when Gramma and I went to Montpelier to live with Dad. A lone giggler is not a happy person; she's a fool. I was still around laughter but not a part of it. My father and his friends told stories and laughed knowingly, and I could only wonder what tickled them. Gramma chuckled at the stories, but I think the humor she and I devised together was more to her liking.

I do not know how she could ever even laugh, being away from home and without Grampa and lonely to the quick. We played cards, canasta mostly, and threw our heads back in real laughter at the game's fate and tricks. We shared a bedroom and a bed, so Gramma never had a chance to sob herself to sleep.

"Peanut, turn over, your little feet are boring holes into my back," she said gently, long after we should have been asleep. "Put your back to mine, now, and we'll toast the air between us."

"Like a piece of bread?"

"Uh-huh."

"Homemade bread?" I asked, since I had her attention.

"Hmmmm."

"Will we butter it and have jam, too?"

By this time I was kneeling on the bed facing Gramma's back.

"You're hungry, Little Rascal," she said observantly.

"I am, I am," I said as I began bouncing on the bed. Gramma was trying to get back to sleep.

Suddenly the bed broke. The slats cracked, the springs crashed to the floor on Gramma's side, and I was thrown on top of her. The commotion and the big thud surely awakened the folks who lived downstairs, as had happened several times before.

Gramma and I could not restrain ourselves in the dark and on the floor. We just broke into sheer laughter. First, we stayed on the floor and enjoyed the only sure salvageable part of the night's event. Then we groped for a light switch to view the damage, and we laughed again. Gramma always started the damage review refrain with a country cussing.

"Dangdarnit, it's broke again."

"Dangdarnit" was as strong a saying as Gramma could come up with, although we both knew and had heard tougher words. "Dangdarnit" just did not cover our situation, so we had to sit on a side rail or a chair, try to squelch our laughter by covering up our mouths with one hand, and hold on to our stomachs with the other.

Sometimes Dad came to help us put the bed together, and that always deserved a laugh, too. He was not skilled at anything domestic, and he was sleepier than we. Gramma and I were fully awake from puffing at the ridiculous, and we had watched him fumble at the task before, which means we built our laughter on the previous laughs.

When the bed was put together (a half hour to do the puzzle), Gramma and I gingerly climbed into it. We had not had bread and jam and butter, and we were cold; but we had smiles on our faces and a good story for the morning.

□

Life was hardly all laughs for Dad in Montpelier. His plate was full, as they say. He may have known by then that his wife was ill beyond recovery and that their love would never be regained. His father, the old pivot of our family wheel, was gone, and Dad was the oldest of his siblings and the only man. He had children to care about alone, a mother he felt he should provide for, and a burdensome "thinking job."

Dad's job was working at a desk and at politics. Years later, I realized he had an important job. He was a state government department head, a member of the governor's cabinet, and a guardian of the new teachers' retirement fund. He worked for a progressive administration wresting power from the old guard, so there was plenty of tension in Dad's work.

I was experiencing my own tension in Montpelier. On the surface the tension was from appearances: I was a country girl in city life. I had two braids hanging amply to my waist that were combed and plaited by Gramma every morning. Braids were rare at the city school. Gramma also outfitted me in dresses with tie-bows in the back, and she scheduled me to wear the same dress for two days in a row. The other girls, more citified, wore skirts and blouses, without a schedule of when to wear them. And they wore white socks, while mine were dark.

Beneath the surface, I felt different from my peers because I was motherless and on the move. No one else seemed to be in the same situation. Divorces, for example, were rare then. There was no questionnaire or study to determine that I was different, but I gleaned the information the sure way — through playground talk.

One day in class something happened that must have shown the teacher that I was experiencing tension in spades. For no apparent reason, I wet my underpants, creating a large puddle on the floor beside my desk. At first, I felt disengaged from the event, as if it had happened to someone else; but shortly afterward I was mortified. The teacher and my fellow students were forgiving and, as I recall, they did not laugh.

They did laugh at me, however, weeks later when the teacher asked us each to stand and say what kind of work our fathers did. (For once, I am grateful for the gender stereotyping of the time. What would I have said about my mother?) Many types of jobs were described: a grocer, quarry miners and stonecutters, a shoe salesman, several kinds of mill workers, a teacher, and a janitor. A janitor . . . I thought of Grampa and wished I could describe his work. Instead, I was in a quandary because I did not really know what my father did for a job.

"Harriet, it's your turn," our teacher said.

I must have looked puzzled and I did not stand up.

"Stand up, now. Tell us what your father does for work."

Suddenly I remembered the one thing I had seen my father do whenever I visited him at his office. I stood up proudly.

"He reads a newspaper," I announced loudly and confidently. "All the time. From the first page to the last."

The class and the teacher roared with laughter. I sat down confused and thought perhaps my father's work was ridiculous.

Whenever I stopped at his office after school, the only thing I ever saw him do was read a newspaper. The afternoon edition had just come out, and he would be leaning back in his chair, resting his feet upon his desk, and reading peacefully to himself. Then he would see me standing in the doorway.

"Well, well, well. Hello there," he said as he dropped the paper to the desk and his feet to the floor. "Come in, Harriet." Dad did not have any pet names for me. But he always had a hug or kiss.

"I was just reading the paper. There's a front-page article about something I am working on. They've got it all wrong, again."

Then Dad chuckled. He motioned for me to sit in a chair across from his desk as if I were his contemporary. He asked me about school, politely, the way adults often comment on the weather to ease into conversation. Then he returned to the newspaper subject as if that were precisely why I was there.

"Things aren't always the way they appear to be, you know. In fact, sometimes they're presented just the opposite of how they really are," he said as he reinstated his feet upon the desk. "Like a mirror."

Then he smiled a big smile, winked at me, and chuckled again. I could tell Dad was still thinking about the newspaper article.

"Remember that," he said, meaning the mirror presenting a reverse image. "It may help you someday."

Dad returned to his reading while I looked out the window or bothered his secretary in the other room. I lingered until he set his paper down; then I asked if he would leave work early and walk me home. Sometimes he did, which gave me lots of time with him because he was a slow walker. Dad always offered his philosophy on life.

"There's two sides to a conversation, you know," Dad said.

"You mean there are two people talking?" I asked as I practically skipped in place because Dad was so slow.

"Nope, I mean there's always got to be one person talking and one listening. Listening is an important part of conversation."

"Yup," I agreed as I bounced and my braids slapped against my back.

"What you do speaks so loud I cannot hear what you say." He quoted one of his favorite maxims. "Now I'm going to show you what I mean about listening and conversation. We'll be silent for a while."

As we walked along in silence, all I could hear was the noise of my own skipping. After a while Dad spoke.

"We were both listening just then. Two listeners at the same time don't make a conversation, just as two talkers don't either," he said.

I laughed at Dad's ability to make his point by example, and he smiled appreciatively that I had understood the reason for the silence. I wondered if his philosophy about conversation was connected to his admonition back in his office about mirrors. I had an image of my father reading the newspaper that had not gotten the story right.

"Then there must be a writer for a reader," I suggested to Dad as I walked backward in front of him so I could see his face.

"And a reader for the writer, too," he said as he cupped both hands to look like an open book and put them in front of his eyes.

I had caught on to Dad's philosophy about opposites, and we exchanged examples while we wound our way home by changing from one side of the street to the other and turning corners. I skipped or walked backward while Dad just ambled straight ahead. It was our philosophical game, entertainment for a lonely man and a lonely girl. We laughed a lot, of course.

□

During our first year in Montpelier, we lived in what I now know was a tenement apartment. The kitchen was a nightmare for Gramma. It was a converted closet with one small window and no view, and we picked up our meals at the stove and walked them down the hallway to the small living room. There is not much worth remembering about the place except the stairway to the outside door, and that is only because it was the way out.

In the summertime Gramma went back to her home, and I was farmed out to my parents' friends or sent to camp. I hated camp. It made my life so unbearable, so lonely, that I telephoned my father as often as I could get a counselor to let me make the call and begged him to come and take me home; but he never did. It must have torn apart his heart to hear his little girl crying on the phone that she was homesick. Homesickness is incurable even if the sufferer goes home, because the fear of separation is still there. It is an illness of the heart, and mine was wiped away only by crying until all the homesick tears were gone. However, there was one benefit to camp: My long braids were cut off so I could comb my hair myself, and in the fall I entered school with what I thought was quite a bob.

That fall, Gramma returned from her summer on the farm, and we moved to a much nicer and larger apartment. It was on the first floor, and it had a bigger kitchen than Gramma had even in her own home, a spacious dining room, and a welcoming little porch with entrances to both rooms. It was ideal for entertaining, and my father and grandmother set about the art immediately. Gramma was a cook par excellence. She was used to feeding a harvest table full of hungry hayers with food and drink so worthy that they rushed out to hard work so they could eat her meals again. I think Gramma enjoyed preparing big meals in Montpelier because it took her mind off her sorrows for short spells. That entertaining may have been the only time she was ever really happy away from her own home.

My dad's part in the entertaining was to invite the guests and host the humor. He asked old college friends and fellow politicians who either worked in the city or passed through occasionally; and they welcomed the conviviality and superb food. Dad practiced what he preached about listening, and he looked the part. His standard conversational pose when seated was to raise his arm over his head, drape it across to the other side, and pull on his ear. It was an unconscious habit, and he exercised it most vigorously during a Vermont story. A Vermont story is a dry piece of humor, usually about a Vermonter and most often told by one, as well. I watched him begin to tug on his ear and smile as someone introduced a story.

"The border patrol had been knocking on Vermont doors up by Canada," a guest began. Everyone was listening and no one interrupted.

"Seems there'd been a change in the state line, and they were informing folks who'd be affected. The patrol knocked on the door of a Vermont farmhouse, and the farmer answered. He told the farmer that Vermont's Legislature had made an agreement with Canada and had gone and changed the line.

" 'Your farm and land are no longer in Vermont,' the patrol officer announced to the farmer."

There was a pause to give the Vermonter in the story time to think.

" 'You mean the house, too?' the farmer asked.

" 'Yes, everything you own.'

" 'And now we live in Canada?' he asked.

" 'Yes, I'm sorry to say.'

" 'Are you sure?' the farmer asked the patrol.

" 'Yes, I'm sure.'

" 'Well, thank goodness,' the farmer said. 'My wife was just saying the other night that she didn't think she could stand another Vermont winter.' "

We all laughed at the Vermont story, and Dad, the attentive host, laughed the longest.

□

Most of the guests at our dining table knew my mother, and many had been in our home when she was hostessing and offering fine fare. The table was a graceful, oblong, shiny mahogany Duncan Phyfe that always reminded me of my mother when I sat at it. While the grown-ups at my father's and grandmother's dinner parties were conversing or laughing, I often daydreamed about my mother shining the table until it glistened like a mirror. I remembered following after her while she did the housework and coming to the dining room and the mahogany table. My mother would begin working up a shine on the dark wood as if she were a sailor polishing a ship's brass. She was energetic and meticulous. I stood at the side of the table with my eyes slightly above the surface and watched her long, bare arm move swiftly, as if it were the mechanism on a train's wheel gaining speed. Her rag moved the white paste around and around in concentric circles until the paste was replaced by a mirrorlike shine. My mother stood back, looked from side to side to be sure she had not missed a spot, and then she smiled with satisfaction. I saw her pretty face reflected in the pretty table as if it were a mahogany-framed mirror — both when I saw her shine it and later as I daydreamed at dinner when I lived without her.

When I was a grown woman, I learned my mother was the real humorist in our family. She was a cutup, a great joke- and story-teller, an ad lib mimic, and a last-minute costume creator. But I did not know that when I lived with her, nor did I hear it from my parents' friends at the table when Dad and Gramma entertained. No one talked about my mother or spoke her name in my presence. Mattie was my mother's name. It is a wonder I remembered it since I had rarely heard it. Oh, occasionally there would be a half-whispered mention of "your mother" to me, but it was unaccompanied by content.

I learned years later, so late it is only worth its weight in feathers, that my mother made people cry from laughing at her antics and funny stories.

"She was full of stories and, oh, so witty," my mother's oldest and best friend (Aunt Marion to me) once said when I was asking her about my mother. "Why, if she heard a story she'd bring it back to us girls and make us laugh and laugh. We could never remember the story well enough to retell it ourselves, but she could recall it immediately and make it even funnier the second time around."

My mother's photograph album, which I did not see until I was an adult, has pictures of her in a Charlie Chaplin outfit: a coat, top hat, and cane. There are three different photographs of Mattie pretending to be Charlie Chaplin, and she smiles a different smile to match each pose. Then below the pictures she has written "Every family has *one*."

Aunt Cynie, my father's sister and the mother of my cousins Liz and Mary, told me about her laughing with my mother.

"I just loved her. She was as funny as anyone I ever knew. When she lived next door to us during the war, and you kids were only knee-high to a grasshopper, she'd come over and make me laugh. She would tell one story after another. I don't know how she could ever remember so many stories, and with all the details."

When my cousins and I were at the height of our giggling, we used to tee-hee ourselves silly at the table, and eventually we were sent away from it. If we had known then that our mothers as grown women were great laughers, too, we could have teased them that they were responsible for our dining-delinquencies. But my mother was not around to tease, which took the fun out of the whole idea. However, I have an image of how much fun they had together from Aunt Cynie's recollections.

"Sometimes your mother would mimic the characters in her stories," she said. "She might don a prop, like using the cover of a laundry basket as her hat, or turn a mop upside down and talk to it. She was all over my kitchen telling her story, and sometimes I fell right on the floor, laughing so until my sides hurt. Well, I'm telling you, we'd laugh until we just plain cried."

Aunt Cynie's kitchen is the same place where Mary did her antics, Liz failed to stop her, and I rolled about the floor the day Grampa was buried. Our laughter was a release from tension, a mirror image of the adults' grief. I often wonder if my mother's great humor — her clowning and her storytelling — was a mirror of her sadness underneath.

□ □ □ □

Summer Ivories

The piano music tinkled up through the floor register to the summer bedroom where Marylin and I stretched our young browned legs atop the sheets before a shaft of moonlight.

"I wish I could stay awake long enough to hear when your Mama stops playing," I whispered to Marylin about the pleasant lady I called Aunt Marion and the tunes she was drawing out of the old upright in the parlor.

"Oh, our daddies will just keep coaxing her for more until I think her fingers must cry to go to sleep," Marylin sighed as she pulled up the sheet to cover our limp bodies.

It was another blissful Vermont summer night with a family that was not mine but who warmed me like their own. During the years when we lived in Montpelier, when I was eight through ten and without a family like Marylin's, I was a constant guest. Friends of my parents were always offering to take me on in the summertime and, as I recall, Dad always acquiesced. There was really little choice. Gramma, who lived with us during my school year, returned to her farm for the summer, and my father insisted I stay with him in Montpelier where he worked.

"No, thank you," he told Gramma when she offered to take me home with her. "She belongs with me. We'll manage." During the late 1940s, single parenting was not fashionable nor often performed by men, so for Dad to have kept me when he knew he could not give me the attention Gramma would have shows he must have been hanging on to me for dear life. All else seemed gone. He was clearly in charge of my summers, keeping in touch by telephone from his work to our home, the way "latch-key" children are often raised, and coming home to cook supper; but he also thought I needed some "fresh air." I refused to go away to camp after my bout with homesickness, so Dad sometimes relied on his old friends to care for me.

Marylin's family, the Hinsdales, lived in Burlington, Vermont's largest city just north of Montpelier. Burlington stretches gracefully along Lake Champlain, the "great lake" of the Northeastern United States, and is the community where both my mother and Aunt Marion grew up and became best friends. They were in the same class at university, lived and worked together for a few years afterward, and then started their own families in homes back in Burlington within what Aunt Marion called "baby-carriage distance." There was something preordained about their friendship: Both women were born on the same day in the same small state. It may have helped my mother when she became ill to trust that her best friend would care about her little family.

The Hinsdales had an old Vermont farmhouse and abandoned barn on a backroad outside Burlington. They spent their summer weekends there and called the vacationing a "resting spell." Marylin's father, Uncle Clark to me, and my father worked in their respective cities during the week, and then drove to the old farmhouse on Friday night for the weekend. Aunt Marion, a pretty woman with blondish wisps around her face and a softness in her voice, often took her children a day or two before the weekend to the farmhouse, and she usually included me. She introduced us to the adult concept of rest by making us tired and hungry from breathing too much country air too fast. We jumped into hay the farmer had left in the barn as if we were acrobatic artists on a trampoline, and we swam in a cool spring-fed pond down the road until the moon threatened to replace the sun.

The Hinsdales' white farmhouse was a series of rooms linked together like the cars of a train, and it rested on a knoll with views of green pastureland, the brown pond, and blue mountains in the distance. It was as still and peaceful as tall marsh grasses in a gentle wind except, of course, for our happy voices and Aunt Marion's evening songs.

"Merry-leen, merry-leen," I called out to Marylin, the blond-haired girl who let me be her younger sister in the summer. I pretended my musical mimic of her name was ringing across the barnyard like sleigh bells. It was a Friday evening, and we were looking for our fathers' cars to raise dust along the old dirt road. "Your Mama's goin' ta teach me somethin' in the kitchen," I shouted from the farmhouse door to Marylin who was on sentry duty to sight our dads. "We're having sliced Elberta peaches for supper," I announced the project with pride.

Aunt Marion set a bowl of peaches as big as baseballs on the wood counter and a pan of boiling water in the long black iron sink with a hand pump on one end. The setting sun cast a pale yellow light in the old narrow kitchen and made my domestic classroom seem washed in gold.

"I peel and you slice," Aunt Marion said as I stood on a small stool to imitate her height. "Take a peeled peach and hold it in your left hand. You're right-handed, aren't you?" She assumed as she gave me a small sharp knife by offering the handle. I was left-handed, but my mother had taught me to write with my right. Perhaps I was working hard to be right-handed for her when she returned.

Quicker than a hummingbird, Aunt Marion dipped the large, pink, furry balls into hot water with a fork. With a paring knife in her other hand, she slipped the whole skin off in two strokes.

"Balance your peach, honey. It's slippery like a baby in a bath. Palm up." She showed me how to hold the golden, moon-shaped, juicy fruit firmly with my thumb and two fingers positioned like a cradle. "Now, slice from the dimple to the bottom. You'll make another slice just like that and another until you've gone all around the peach."

The process was a marvel to me. The peach kept slipping, but I kept returning the project to my hand. I made a dozen yellow quarter moons with burgundy etched on the inside curves until all I held was the nutlike pit with carved swirls.

I waned halfway through the peach project and watched Aunt Marion finish our jobs with a motion like the figure eight. First she brought the peach from the counter down into the sink to dip it into the hot water, then up to peel it, then down to rinse it in a bowl of cool water, and then back up to place it on the counter and pick up another peach to peel — without breaking her rhythm or the figure eight. She was a skilled teacher, letting the student watch as well as work to keep up the excitement that goes with newness.

Aunt Marion was, in fact, a teacher by profession, as was my mother. The two women had taught school before each was married and lived with two other female teachers in what, I later learned, were years of great fun and bliss. After they were both married, Aunt Marion and my mother linked up Uncle Clark and my father and their children in their special friendship. If I wanted to get close to my mother — and I did — then Aunt Marion was the best and only surrogate: She kept our families together gracefully and deftly, the way she peeled peaches in a figure eight.

"Now we give the fruit something sweet and sour," Aunt Marion explained as she squeezed a half a lemon from one hand and followed with sugar dropping from the other.

When the men arrived for the weekend, Dad and I hugged more often than all the other huggers put together, as if proving two could make a family as well as four. Aunt Marion served up supper on the outstretched pine drop-leaf table and made a fuss about dessert.

"Harriet made our sweet tonight," she almost sang as she set the blue willowware bowl of peaches on the table and put her free hand on my shoulder. "It'll be the best you've tasted all summer."

The sweetest thing that happened to me all summer was not the dessert but what wafted in the air when we went to bed. Aunt Marion would offer, or be persuaded, to play the upright piano angled across a corner of the parlor while the men sat silently and mused. We children went to bed willingly because the best was yet ahead. Aunt Marion played songs from sheet music spawned by World War II and old tunes that she sometimes decorated with her clear voice.

Marylin and I lay quietly. We watched the crescent of the new moon get brighter as the night got darker and prepared to dream in music instead of being stalked by ghoulish images that children often see.

"Some day I'm gonna play music like your mama, Merryleen," I told my friend my deepest wish.

"To keep the bogeyman away, I bet," she whispered. Marylin understood.

My childish wish grew with me. First I hammered out scales and little Thompson ditties. Then I mastered "Für Elise" and sheet music of the 1950s. The urge lay fallow until I had children of my own and an old upright in my own home's parlor.

What to do with children? It came so naturally. I remembered Aunt Marion's example. Give them a place to run — to breathe fresh air fast — and lead them to a place to swim. Feed them fruit. Show them how it is peeled and sugared. Love all children as if they were your own. Then, just before they go to sleep, give them music by the silvery moon.

□

The Mitchells were my other summer family. "Uncle Bob" Mitchell and my father shared a common grief: loss of spouse, Uncle Bob's to death and Dad's to mental illness; and two children each to raise alone. Uncle Bob remarried but did not forget his old friend's need. He shared his new family life by often taking me in at his summer cottage on Lake Dunmore in Vermont. It was an idyllic arrangement for me because his oldest child, Margie, was eleven when I was nine and, although she added a year as regularly as I did, she never let me lag behind.

Margie was Uncle Bob's girl, anyone could see. He was tall and attractive, sandy-haired with freckles, and bespectacled. Margie was pretty with paper-white skin, freckles everywhere, and dark auburn hair. I used to think Margie would grow to be like her father in every way except gender because at an early age she imitated his profession as well as his looks.

Uncle Bob was a newspaper man who became Vermont's "journalism dean," and Margie was a master storyteller for someone her age. Not a liar, mind you, but a skilled entertainer with words. She could build a story after supper the way an old woman can turn a ball of yarn into something warm to wear without looking at her hands. Margie told stories to her younger brother, John, and me while we squeaked the swinging couch on their front porch and listened to the water lap against the small sand beach.

"Give me a start," Margie began with the confidence that she could manufacture anything. "Whatcha wanna hear about?"

"Tell about a woolly bear," John piped up from his corner of the couch.

Margie gazed off at the dusky waters of Lake Dunmore to fill her mind with John's idea and then looked at us with two huge eyes that seemed to have seen everything.

"Once upon a time, on the road that comes into our camp, lived an old man in a little homemade hut. He made it from fallen limbs and filled the holes with moss and autumn leaves. Every spring before we'd come, he'd tear it down so we would not know he lived here."

"Ah, come on Margie," John challenged her opening lines. "No one lives around here in winter."

"Oh, yes, brother dear. You can see the stones he uses for an outdoor fireplace up beside our road. It's just he's scattered them to fool us."

Margie's explanation gave her full charge of the ensuing story except for our exclamations of "yikes" and "what a monster!" She kept us rapt with details about the old man who raised two cubs to full-grown bears, how he fought and killed with his bare hands the one that dared to maul him, and about the breakup of the "Dunmore Den." Margie strung out her story until the lake was dark and the electric lights were turned on inside the cottage.

"Well, what happened to the old man and the bear that's left?" John asked as he got up to leave the couch.

"They're still wandering," Margie answered, "but not to-gether. They went their separate ways. Each circles Lake Dunmore afraid to meet the other."

"Okay, Margie, I liked your story, but you never said nothing about the bear being woolly. Huh? Huh?" John announced as he walked barefoot across the dark porch to go inside. "I said I wanted to hear about a WOOLLY bear," he shouted as he opened the screen door.

"Just a moment," Margie said calmly without turning to look at John. "You can feel the woolly with your own feet. The bear rug by Daddy's chair? That's the skin of the cub that grew mean."

Margie had a way of making her stories take on reality long after they were spun. Plus, she taught John and me how to spin our own tales.

"Start with one idea," Margie instructed me. "Tell me all about it. And your story doesn't need to end any certain way or time. Make it last like summer."

"Like summer?" I wondered if there were some trick to continuing the happiness of Lake Dunmore forever. "School ends summer," I reminded her.

"Not in your imagination," Margie answered with the look of a wise old woman.

One summer my visit to the Mitchells ended abruptly. Margie and I were innocently skipping stones before a swim. We were deep in conversation and knee-deep in the water as we searched for flat skippers in the shoal. I reached down to dip out what I must have thought a "winner," and when I stood up to cast my stone upon the water, something struck me across the face. It was blinding. There was a whirling siren in my head and the sight of stars in many colors. Margie had thrown a stone the moment I stood up and had lost her aim, striking my mouth full force at close range. It was a mistake, a childish misjudgment about time and space.

My front teeth were shattered and I bled profusely. Uncle Bob rowed me and my armful of bloody towels across Lake Dunmore to a doctor in less time than he thought it would take to circle the lake by car. But he had not counted on the storm that hit when we were halfway across the water. Poor Uncle Bob. He kept talking lightheartedly to give me confidence while he arched his back to give the oars his best.

"You'll be all right," he said while looking over his shoulder to chart a course without a landmark. "At least you won't have to pull those baby teeth."

"Bees arnt baby beef," I spoke through my fat lips. "Bear my grown-up beef," I tried to explain by flashing two fingers.

The doctor reset the loosened teeth and cleaned out the chips hiding between my swollen lips and gums. One tooth, a prominent incisor, was split up the middle, and two lower teeth had lost their "bite-ability." Eventually, years of dentists' fingers, files, and drills softened the sawed-off teeth and fashioned a capped tooth to mark my smile.

Margie and I rarely saw each other after the broken teeth episode — not because the accident had split our friendship but because Dad, Gramma, and I soon moved to Kansas City, fifteen hundred miles away from Vermont and our old friends. When we returned to Vermont the next two summers, Margie and I had less in common because we had lost touch and could not overcome the two years' difference in age as easily as before, so I only visited the Mitchells for a few days. The end of my summer families had coincided with my broken teeth.

I was surprised that Margie did not grow up to become a writer like her father. John and I both pursued "written word" careers as if to prove we had learned our lessons well. Instead of emulating her father, Margie became an investment banker like my father. There is imagination in that field, but it must touch reality frequently.

"Ah, yes, that's Margie," John might well say if he remembers the woolly bear story and the camp rug.

So, thanks to Margie, I carry a little touchstone of summer in my mouth, something to spark my imagination. Just a thumb-rub across my ivories, like a swift finger run along piano keys, reminds me that I was often fostered by parents other than my own. Those few Vermont summers, and the earlier ones with my grandparents, were as idyllic as any summers I have ever known.

□ □ □ □

CHAPTER 10

The Amulet

Afew weeks before Christmas in 1950, when I was almost eleven years old, we moved from Vermont to Kansas City, Missouri. Gramma and I took a two-day train trip to join my father, who had a new job in Kansas City and had found us a place to live. Everything Gramma and I experienced, from eating in the dining car to sleeping in a compartment, was new to us. Porters, big stations like Chicago's where we changed trains, and the flat terrain made us feel like strangers before we even arrived. But we had each other.

Or so I thought. Urbanity and my father's new style of living were quite a shock to Gramma, and I imagine she was in a quandary about whether or not she would stay from the first moment she saw our new home. Dad had taken rooms in an apartment hotel, ideal perhaps for a busy bachelor but hardly suitable for a country lady like Gramma who intended to keep house for us by cooking up a storm and hanging laundry on a line. Dad's rooms did not even include a kitchen. There was a refrigerator on a sun porch but no sink or stove. We took our meals in the grand hotel dining room, which sported linen, silver, fresh flowers, and waiters who served and cleared from different sides. The hotel personnel, except for the owners, were mostly black people and the roomers were all white people. In the garage beneath the apartments, a uniformed attendant brought around one's car when called, and would wash and shine it for a slightly extra charge. Gramma did not drive a car, of course, so such a service was useless for her. To Gramma's mind, any service was useless. She was in a place with nothing for her to do, so she simply "upped and out."

I was stunned and devastated that she would leave when we had just arrived. I felt betrayed or tricked. Had Gramma ever really intended to stay? Did she only take the train trip to get me out there? Was I just so much baggage to be delivered? I am not sure that as a child I ever cried in the daylight over the loss of my mother, although I had nightmares for years; but I bawled at Gramma's leaving. My separations from Gramma and my mother were a study in contrasts: Gramma had traveled a great distance to drop me off and then she left voluntarily, whereas my mother had traveled to retrieve me and then been dragged away.

The night before Gramma left, a few days before Christmas, we said good-bye to each other in our bedroom. We cried together. We were sitting on our bed, and Gramma tried to make us laugh instead of cry by bouncing lightly on the thing to see if it would collapse. I could not even pretend to giggle. Gramma and I had never been sad together, and it seemed like a dark pit we would never get out of without someone else's help. Then Gramma pulled a package wrapped in Christmas paper out of a dresser drawer and handed it to me.

"This is your Christmas present, but you might as well have it. No need to save it. I won't be here, and you need the lift now."

I tried to stop sobbing to comply with Gramma's intentions while I unwrapped her gift. It was a foot-high, stuffed deer with yellow fur and pink cheeks.

"It's probably not grown-up enough a present for you," Gramma said as I held the stuffed animal straight in front of my face so I could look directly into its glass eyes. It was not a fair trade —a pretend deer for a real grandmother— but I realized the pet and I would have to try to make it work.

"I'm leaving you in good care, Little One," Gramma said as she packed. "Your schooling is down the way. You're old enough to walk alone. There's nothing here for me to do except to go raving mad. You'll come home to me this summer, and we'll repair whatever damage's been done."

When Gramma left, the hotel lost one of its younger residents. The clientele was so old that my dad was the next to youngest by decades, and I was so much the very youngest that the cane-supported oldsters considered me their pet. I had eighty grandparents if I needed one. No wonder Gramma thought I had "care a-plenty."

Schooling in Kansas City was as much a shock for me as the living conditions had been for Gramma. Dad had enrolled me in a Roman Catholic convent school for girls, located at the far end of the wide, green parkway that ran in front of our hotel. The school was mammoth. The front doors made such an impression on me that they still represent the "power of Kansas City" in my imagination. They were large halves of a high arch, like a giant walnut, which when opened could let in four abreast. The doors had clean shiny windows set in lead panes that sparkled as much as the polish on the dark wood frames. I walked through the impressive front entrance only once: when I was admitted after Christmas for the next term.

The center hallway had a marble floor and a two-story winding staircase. It looked like a state capitol or a large hotel, every bit the opposite of my country schoolhouse. The Mother Superior's offices were on the right, a complex I never entered; and, the receptionist's little office was on the left, a place where I spent many hours with a nun who tutored me in French, the second language spoken daily in the convent.

The convent school was run by a French order of nuns for a hundred privileged Catholic girls. The black-robed women rustled down the hallway like breezes blowing leaves. A girl named Lucy and I were the only Protestant students in the school, and we soon gravitated to each other. I spoke only English where bilingualism

was expected so I felt out of place with the other students immediately, and I never overcame the feeling of intimidation or my
awe. Day students came in chauffeur-driven limousines and, although I played with the girls at recess inside the high iron fence
around the school yard, I never saw them in their homes nor in
my hotel rooms. There were a few boarding students who slept on
cots divided by curtains in the upstairs of the convent. Once, when
I was ill at school and resting on an upstairs bed, I saw how they
lived. In the cold, severe cubicles, there was only enough space for
slippers by an iron bed. I thought that to be a boarder one must
be a Catholic and that my being Protestant was, in this case, a
stroke of luck.

There was nothing joyful about the experience for me. There
were perks such as ballet and tap dancing but in these, as in every
other nonacademic pursuit, I was years behind. Although I stayed
through the school year, I determined early on that public school
was more my match and told my father so immediately.

While the girls in my class took catechism, I took French with
Sister Alphonsina in the little office by the front entrance across
from the Mother Superior's office. Sister Alphonsina doubled as
the receptionist while she tutored me, and I grew to appreciate
that she was a true gatekeeper. I soon stopped feeling like a
stranger when I was with her because she was always jumping up
to greet a visitor and returning to me as if I were her old friend.
Sister Alphonsina turned out to be my best and only friend at the
convent. She was French, and I think she welcomed a little listener
whom she could tell about her home. We conjugated verbs and
talked about almost everything in her native tongue, including my
"verts monts."

"Nous ne parlons qu' en francais," Sister Alphonsina insisted
quietly if I slipped into "anglais."

She told me stories about her childhood and abbey life in
France. Sister Alphonsina was the oldest nun at the convent and
rather wizened, and I worried that she would die in Kansas City
and never get back to France, even in a casket. Perhaps she worried

about me, too, since I felt I was in a strange land and lived outside the convent's great walnut doors.

□

When I landed in Kansas City, I might just as well have been dropped off on the Planet Mars and told I would never again see anyone I had known before, except my father and "Aunt Nancy." Aunt Nancy, whom I had met in Vermont when she was there on vacation, was not our relative, but she had more influence on our lives in the Kansas City years than all my father's and my relations combined. First of all, Aunt Nancy was the reason we were living there. She was president of a company and had hired my father as its vice president. Then she planned where we should live, where I should attend school, and our evening entertainment. Aunt Nancy was my father's social friend as well as his boss, and they usually took me along to dine out or at her home, a big house with servants who often fed me and entertained me. So life in Kansas City was as far removed from my life in Vermont as being an alien on Mars.

"Living on Mars" must have distanced me from the realities of how my mother figured in our lives. My father was still married to her, so I most likely believed she would someday return to us. A divorce simply never occurred to me, partly because I did not understand such arrangements. Therefore, I reasoned that Aunt Nancy must be temporary in our lives, which made her company easy on my preadolescent psyche. But I lied to people who inquired about my mother's whereabouts or commented that I must miss her.

"Oh, it doesn't bother me," was my stock answer for both the questions and the commentaries. I construed any conversation about my mother, even a simple reference, as a camouflaged interrogation about my feelings. I was as defensive and deceiving as someone with contraband would be at immigration. One old person at the hotel spoke kindly to me about my mother's absence, and I quickly gave her my manufactured answer and a smile. She must have passed the word among the other residents that family talk was useless with their little pet because no one at the hotel ever brought it up again. My pat reply was equally successful in deflecting curiosity from my peers.

I put my energy and new independence to work to overcome the "stranger" factor at school. Students at the convent wore navy blue uniforms so I at least looked like them. There was nothing to differentiate us except cordons and medals. The cordon was a wide green, grosgrain ribbon that stretched diagonally from a girl's shoulder to her waist, and since it represented academic honors, only a small percentage of the students sported them. There were single cordons for high marks and double ones for the highest grades. The girls mounted pins for special awards on their cordons. The cordon-decked students looked like little generals roaming the convent halls, and I coveted the look. Since the awards were given out only twice a year — at Christmastime and in June — and I had entered after Christmas, I had nothing distinctive to wear on my uniform. Although I earned a single cordon (without pins) at the end of the year, the achievement was anticlimactic because it was the last day of school and I was not coming back.

The girls had devised another way to distinguish themselves individually. They wore chains around their necks that dangled little oval or round, silver-colored things as thin as dimes — religious medals. Each medal had some saint's image stamped on it and Latin words around the edges. I studied each classmate's collection as regularly as I studied French. A girl carefully kept her chain of medals outside her blouse so it would make a jangling noise when she played or ran down the winding staircase. I thought that popularity was based more on how many medals a student wore than on her personality or cordons or pins. A large collection — seven or eight silver saints dangling from a necklace — made the greatest noise, and I learned to estimate from the sound of the swinging musical amulets the social worth of a girl as if I were tapping a glass to hear if it was crystal.

Sister Alphonsina gave me a medal, perhaps out of understanding or as a reward for conjugating French verbs. Lucy, the other Protestant student, and I once met on a Saturday and took the trolley car downtown to look for shiny little amulets in the dime store. We found religious medals between the jewelry and the barrettes, and I bought two and donned them immediately. The charms jangled against each other when I skipped, and I felt very "Catholic."

Chapel attendance was required daily. The French nuns sang Gregorian chants from a balcony in the back, the Mother Superior made announcements from the front, and we spent a lot of time in silence. Except for kneeling, it was familiar to me because my Methodist experience with Gramma had consisted mostly of women congregating for silence and singing.

I often wondered what the girls learned in catechism while I studied French, but I only felt excluded from their religion once. The Bishop came for a big service in the chapel, and it was rumored he would pass out medals. The occasion was different from daily chapel primarily because there was a man in the midst of our female congregation. He was dressed in white and gold and was very active all alone in the front of the chapel, chanting and gesticulating. I watched carefully as the first rows of students went up to kneel before him.

He walked along the line of bowed heads and gave each girl something. I assumed he was handing out the promised medals and became quite excited. But when it came our row's turn to go up front, two girls spun around and said I could not go.

"You're a Protestant," one hissed.

"So what!" I said and pushed ahead. The girls on the aisle would not let me through, and someone pushed me back down onto the pew. I felt embarrassed and cheated as the others went up front and knelt to receive the Bishop's gift.

The Bishop was passing out wafers for communion, of course, but I did not know that. As we filed out of chapel, he stood at the door and shook each hand including mine. I felt a cold hole in my sweaty palm. He smiled sweetly and gave me a medal just as he was giving every other girl.

☐

My father, who was not a Catholic, had sent me to the convent school under pressure from Aunt Nancy, so he yielded easily when I asked to leave at the end of the year.

"I don't care where you go to school," he told me, "as long as you're learning. And I don't care what religion you take up with, either, just so it's one of your own choice."

Something happened, however, at the convent that impressed him mightily. One evening, he attended a parents' meeting with the Mother Superior. He came home with a story he could hardly believe, a story that he often told for the next thirty years.

The Mother Superior was an imposing character: tall and broad and quite erect. When she walked the convent's halls, she was always a few steps ahead of the sisters, who seemed small compared to her, and the air moved ahead of her like the engine of a train. She was authority personified, and she made the greatest noise of all the nuns because of her rosary, which had beads as large as chips of coal and jangled from somewhere within the folds of her big black robe.

During World War II, as my father told her story, the Mother Superior was head of an abbey in France, and she had many nuns in her charge. The Germans had occupied the nearby village, and she learned that they were pillaging and raping and had the latter on their minds for the women in her abbey. The Mother Superior kept the threatening information to herself to prevent hysteria.

Late one night while the nuns were sleeping, a German officer led his men up the hill to the abbey. The Mother Superior was waiting for them. She opened the doors of the abbey, stood in the doorway so they could see her as they approached, and then stretched her arms across the entrance when they arrived. She must have been a great black bulwark in the abbey door.

"You shall not cross my threshold, except over my dead body," she told the marauders. Perhaps the silver cross on the Mother Superior's black rosary flashed in the night like an amulet.

"You will have to rape me first," she threatened the officer, "before the eyes of God."

The Germans turned tail and the sisters slept on.

When my father told the story, I envisioned the Mother Superior standing in the front entrance of my convent school in Kansas City. I can still see the image: The great halves of the arched doorway are open as in the perfect splitting of a dark walnut, and she is standing in full form with her black robes suspended from her arms stretched across the entrance. A white arch of linen shines around her ruddy face like a repeat of the arched doorway, and she sparkles against the building like an oval medal flashing on a student's chest. The black coallike beads of her rosary dangle from her robes, and I know they will ring when she moves away.

On my final afternoon at the convent, when I was strutting around the halls with the single cordon across my chest, Sister Alphonsina called me to her empty classroom. I knew she had been with the Mother Superior at the abbey in France. I could tell when I sat in Sister Alphonsina's little office and the Mother Superior called across the hall for some paper or an errand that the two women were old friends who had deeper ties than just the same religion. Perhaps the Sister felt eternally grateful to the Mother for her life. I guessed that living inside the convent school was similar to living inside the abbey in France, and I sensed that, with the same woman in charge, Sister Alphonsina must have felt protected from the problems of the outside world no matter where she lived. I was sure, at the least, that I would have liked having the same woman in charge of my life as I moved from place to place.

Sister Alphonsina encouraged me to keep working at my French and wished me well in public school. The good-bye hurt because we both knew we would never see one another again unless I visited the convent, an unlikely possibility. She pulled open a desk drawer and drew out a string of beads.

"A rosary to take with you," she said in English.

Sister Alphonsina showed me how to hold each bead and say a prayer. Sitting beside my old French friend, I memorized "Hail

Mary" instead of conjugating verbs. She was not attempting a conversion because it was too late for that. Perhaps she had waited until the end of my stay so I would not feel coerced, or maybe she thought I had felt left out while the others studied catechism. Her intention was a mystery to me, but I did not analyze it for motives. I simply trusted, as we said au revoir, that she was giving me her order's amulet.

CHAPTER 11

□ □ □ □

Mother Nature
and the Catamount

The two years after I left the convent school seemed to whiz by like wild animals chasing prey. Dad and I were always on the move. We changed residences two more times in Kansas City and returned to Vermont for summers. Our cross-country trips were a vision in double speed. Dad drove me east, dropped me off at Gramma's or at friends', returned to Kansas City, and then drove back to Vermont to pick me up and take me back to Kansas City to start school. That was six thousand miles a summer in a 1950 green Plymouth for Dad. Back and forth, back and forth. We were "perpetual returnees."

Gramma returned to Kansas City the fall I entered sixth grade. I do not know what possessed her to come again, but I was mighty happy. Perhaps she came because our living situation then was more homelike than the hotel rooms she had spurned. Dad had rented a small house on the other side of the city that was closer to his work and near a public school for me. We were also near a Congregational church, which Gramma liked, and she and I walked to attend it every Sunday.

Gramma was not happy, though. I think she came only to make a home life for me. I was not privy to whatever agreements she and Dad had made for her length of stay, but suddenly she was gone again. I accepted her second leaving like peeling skin after a bad sunburn: Some discomfort was resurrected but far less than the initial pain.

While Gramma was taking care of me, I was allowed to adopt a cat and to begin piano lessons on a small rented spinet. The cat was my best friend, and the piano filled up the empty times when the cat was napping or foraging.

After Gramma left, the cat replaced her in my bed. One early morning, I awakened to its meowing under the bedcovers at the foot. When I pulled back the sheet and blankets to rescue her, I saw a pool of blood and two creatures that looked like infant rats. At first I thought my cat had dragged baby rats into our bed and killed them at my feet. Upon closer inspection I realized that the tiny, warm corpses were her newborn kittens. Dad helped me clean the mess up. Silly me, I thought. I did not know an infant kitten when I saw one, and I did not even know my cat was pregnant. I was biologically illiterate at age twelve.

☐

The next year, Dad moved us back to the residential hotel and invited his youngest sister, a secretary by trade, to live with us and work. My aunt, who was barely old enough to have a child my age, and I shared a bedroom as Gramma and I had always done, but not a bed. She worked, sewed her own wardrobe, and developed a social life.

Both the cat and the spinet piano were moved to the hotel, and they kept me company after school. I took a trolley car across the city to my old public school and home again each day. I spent my life going back and forth — across the city in trolley cars or across a plain landscape to Vermont — or being completely still and lonely in the empty hotel rooms when Dad and my aunt were working. I did not make lasting friends my own age in Kansas City because I was never in a place near my peers long enough.

However, I made a good friend of the man who ran the garage in the hotel basement just beneath our rooms. When I got off the trolley after school, I went straight to see him the way I had gone to see Grampa in his barn. When I arrived, my cat would be with the garage man, rubbing up against his black chauffeur suit pants, or it would come through a hole in the garage wall when it heard my voice. The hotel owners had bent their rules about pets by allowing me to have a cat, and they had even created a cat door to our rooms from the garage by having a hole drilled through the concrete foundation and the brick siding. She was the only animal the head chauffeur welcomed in his immaculate work space. It did not seem to matter to him or to the owners that my dad did not even use the garage services. He parked his green Plymouth on the street.

"Hi, Kitten," the garage man greeted me nearly every day after school.

I do not remember my cat's name or the name of the garage man, but the first was gray-colored and the second was black. My human friend was tall and thin, and he put on his chauffeur's hat and suit jacket when he left the garage to take a car around to the front door or when the hotel owners entered his domain. Otherwise, while my furry friend and I watched him wash and polish the big black cars, he was without a hat or jacket and his white shirt sleeves were rolled up.

"Puss, here, he's been bothering me aaallll day." My friend drew out the "all" to tease me as he scrubbed the white walls of a Cadillac's tires.

"Yeah, I know, but you're company for her and she's company for you," I said as I held my cat and stroked her ears. "It's a she-cat, you know, not a he."

"Is that so?" he asked as he swirled his head around to see what I was leading up to.

"Yup, she's already had kittens," I said conclusively. "But they died."

"Well, I'm sorry they died, Kitten, but I know you. If there'd been extras you'd be begging me to take 'em home. And this Puss, he's here all day, and that's enough."

The time came when I had to ask my friend a favor greater than taking kittens home. My father and I would be returning to Vermont in June, this time as "permanent returnees." I could not take my cat. Something had happened to change the course of my life irrevocably. I had only the one friend, a tall man whom I knew I would never see again, to tell about my loss and my father's gain.

"We're going back to Vermont to live," I told the garage man. "In just two weeks."

"I heard," he answered with his back to me as he rinsed a car.

"Did you hear why?" I asked.

"Uh-huh."

"Who told you?" I wondered out loud.

"The hotel owners. They'll be renting your rooms to someone else and closing up the cat door. I needed to know so I can get something to seal up the hole."

"When did you hear?" I asked.

"When did you hear, Kitten?" he answered me with a question and slight turn of head so I could see the side of his eye, and I knew he could see me.

"Last night. My aunt told me."

"Uh-huh."

There was a long silence except for the water splashing on the concrete floor. I never said it and he never said it, but the unspoken was about my father's gain. He was going to marry a woman in Vermont whom I had never met, and his new family included me but not my cat.

I had also just learned that Dad had divorced my mother. I wondered if she had heard he was remarrying when she was notified of the divorce the way I learned of the divorce when I was told about the marriage. How come I had to have another "mother"? I had already had three: my own, my paternal grandmother, and a paternal aunt who was more the age of an older sister than a mother. I was thirteen and tired of mothers: They all came and went or, in the case of the first one, were taken away.

My friend poured a pail of dirty water toward the drain in the center of the floor and set his rags and pail down as he turned toward me.

"You'll have a family, now, Kitten. Someone to look after you all the time." He was standing a few feet away from me and giving me his full attention.

But I was family to my cat, and now I had to abandon her. I was torn, not because I did not want to return to Vermont but because I had to. I rather liked my independence, which was like my cat's coming and going through the little door, and I loved my cat.

"Well, Kitten, is there something you want me to do?" my nice friend asked.

"Yes, but I don't think you'll do it," I said as I scanned the garage to find my gray, furry friend.

"Try me."

"Would you keep my cat?" I finally blurted out as tears poured down my face.

He stepped toward me and wrapped his long strong arms around to hold me while I cried against his chest.

"Of course, Kitten," he said as he gently pushed my hair back behind my ears. "I've already asked my family if they'd take him if you wanted, and they said yes."

"Her," I corrected him and then laughed.

"Him or her. It doesn't matter. We'll call it 'Kitten' after you."

☐

Our last drive back to Vermont seemed to be my final chance to have Dad's company solely to myself. We had lived alone together with intermittent relatives for five years, and the two of us had been the constant of my original family. I thought we had been saving a place for my mother's return the way two people flank a theater seat to save it for their late-arriving friend. I wanted to talk to my father about my mother, but I did not dare break the spell: He was as happy as I could ever remember, so I made a blind bargain that if I was quiet his happiness might rub off onto me. I was panicked that if I did not conform — accept the given of a stepmother and another move — I might lose him, too. The panic was internally produced, not caused by anything he had implied or said. I suffered from lack of communication about my mother.

Dad talked happily about our future. He would be taking on a new job in stocks and bonds, and I would be taking on, once again, a new school. Dad said he hoped I would like his wife-to-be, and he was sure that I, too, would be happy to be back in Vermont.

"I think it's the most beautiful place in the world," Dad said as he pressed on the Plymouth's gas pedal to chase along some flat turnpike. It took three days of driving above the speed limits to travel from Kansas City to Vermont. After years of crisscrossing, we knew the different limits, the states by their terrain, the names of the long mountain underpasses as we neared the East, and the costs of all the tolls.

"When you grow up, you'll be glad to have Vermont as your address." Dad continued on the theme of beauty in our home state.

I asked him why.

"It's the Green Mountain State. There's mostly countryside and lots of mountains, and it's not commercial. It's on Lake Champlain, which is really a sea, it's so big. Vermont is often called 'God's Country,' and lots of people want to buy a piece of it." He pressed on the gas pedal again so he could get to the place he was talking about faster. "And the people are as fine as any you'll ever know," he concluded his promotion.

I was not really listening to my father's chattering about the merits of Vermont or its beauty or my long-range future. In fact, each reference to what we were moving toward put a greater distance between my mother and me as if watching something disappear in a rearview mirror. I was losing hope of ever reconnecting with her. How would she know where to find me, I worried, if she was not married to my father?

Simultaneously, I was trying to piece together my immediate future based on what I already knew like reading road signs up ahead. The woman Dad was going to marry was the widow of one of his best friends. She was a Vermonter, which he seemed to think was all the recommendation anyone would need. We would move into her house in Bennington the very moment we arrived. The next week Dad would marry her, and while they honeymooned I would stay with our new relatives: a woman who would be my stepsister, her husband, and their child.

Here I am, I thought, a thirteen-year-old girl who has been losing family regularly for years, and suddenly I am being rushed to take on new family in just one week. I had been empty for so long, so starved for family life, that the prospect of a giant feast — a marriage and new relatives — made me queasy.

My mother came up only once in our cross-country conversations.

"Your mother didn't, ummm, doesn't seem to be, well, what shall I say?" Dad paused as he rolled his window down and then halfway back up. "She's not getting any better," he finally said.

I said nothing.

I was abundantly confused, and he was awkward talking about the matter, which must be why he had my aunt tell me there would be a shift in his wives.

"I've divorced her. You know that?"

"Yes," I said.

"Do you know why?"

I assumed it was because he did not love her anymore, but I would not come right out and say that. Instead I answered no.

"The law in Vermont says that if your spouse is a patient in a mental hospital for six continuous years then you may automatically divorce her."

I listened and counted back silently through my years to age seven.

"I don't think she'll ever get out of there. I could not wait forever. I, uh, I hope you understand," Dad said sadly.

I loved my father very much so I accepted his explanation, and I felt sorry for the lonely man. But speeding toward Vermont, the promised land of such beauty, and listening to Dad's equation about divorcing my mother to marry another Vermonter planted a seed in my imagination. A sense of place, my home state, began to replace my mother, Mattie, for me. Dad and I were leaving behind a plain terrain and a lonesome existence; and in order to return to something more beautiful and less lonely, we were making a trade: my mother for Vermont.

I felt as helpless at age thirteen moving toward a new step-mother as I had been at age seven when my mother was taken away. I had no choice! So I chose something internally for myself: a new name. I ran through the alphabet silently, repeatedly for two days, until I found a name I liked: Peggy.

I reasoned that my old name had been the cause of our bad luck because I felt responsible for our failed family. I did not think it was my fault that my parents were divorced, as children often feel; no, it was worse than that. I thought it was my fault that my mother was put away, which had led to what appeared to be her permanent incarceration and, now, this irrevocable divorce. If I had not left my mother on that fateful day when Dad took my brother and me away from her, when my mother called my name and warned me she would come and get me if I did not stay with her, then she would not have had to come up in blackberry season to retrieve me at my grandparents' farm. I had not gone to her that day, either, when she screeched for help on the back porch, so I reasoned that the last six years of our torn-apart family were my doing. I still had the child's belief that magic was a useful tool, so I chose the only way I could independently design my new life — a new name, a new me.

I was always glad to get back to Vermont, and that final return was no different. There were just a few miles to drive from the New York border to Bennington, and Dad and I relished the view. It was beautiful! Dad drove slowly for a change. Lime green pastureland poured out of the dark green hardwoods, and in the distance blue-green mountains stood against a range of bigger purple mountains that rolled behind the horizontal hues of green like a giant serpentine. It was early evening in Vermont, and Dad and I had our final ten minutes alone.

"I won't stop loving you, you know, Harriet, just because I'm getting married. You'll always be my favorite girl."

Gee, I thought, he said that just in time. Why did he wait until the last moment? We could have waxed upon the subject for three days and across seven states. I knew, though, that Dad was a true Vermonter because he kept his feelings to himself. Perhaps he had not thought to express his familial love until he saw what he thought was perfect natural beauty.

☐

The introduction to my new home and stepmother was pleasant in every way. First of all, her big, white-painted, brick house had a name above its front door that was an answer to all our wanderings: "Settledown." Secondly, the "mistress" of Settledown, my stepmother-to-be, was welcoming and gracious. She and my father were so happy to see each other that I found their happiness surprisingly infectious.

I was dressed in shorts and a sleeveless blouse when I met my stepmother on her front steps. I entered her home without a suitcase or any other possessions in my hands and felt as I had when I started life at my grandparents' farm: almost naked and prepared to start anew.

Her house was beautiful. Its interior was filled with Oriental rugs and antique furniture, books and Early American porcelain and pottery, framed photographs and paintings, and slightly faded patterned coverings upon the walls and chairs. She had lived in this lovely home for thirty years, and the home itself looked like a pretty, well-dressed matron in her prime.

She took me to the bedroom that would be mine, all mine alone, a sunny little second-story space with an attached enclosed porch where she kept the largest collection of flowering geraniums I had ever seen. I looked over the porch railing to a large green lawn, an English garden with a trellised entrance, and then beyond to the side of a mountain. It was the first time I had ever lived right next to a mountain, and I fancied I would like that.

"This was my daughter's bedroom when she was growing up. She was very happy here. I hope you will be, too," my almost stepmother said assuringly as she opened a closet door to show where my clothes would go. Then she smiled at me and said, "Oh, Dearie, I'm so happy to have another little girl." I learned later that "Dearie" was her favorite affectionate expression, and she had used it with me from the very start.

The first morning at my new home in Bennington, I awakened to find a pool of blood in my bed. It reminded me of my cat in Kansas City who gave birth to kittens beneath my bedding. But here I slept without my cat and realized I must have made the mess myself. It was my first menstruation, for which I was prepared only by knowing what it was. My stepmother helped me sort out the mess, but I thought, what a way to start out with a new mother and a new room. As I look back, I understand it was a rite of passage, and it seems as if Mother Nature herself had orchestrated the timing: I bled for ten days straight, right through the wedding day, and at the end I felt exhausted as well as purged of being motherless and on the move.

☐

The greatest pleasure in my new home was a resident bulldog and an ancient cat. The cat was past enjoying being petted, but the funny-looking bulldog was as sweet and affectionate as any animal I had ever hugged.

Within a day or two I met the neighbor children who all called me Peggy. One girl, Sally, a year younger than I, fast became my friend. It was as satisfying finally to have a constant friend as it was to have a family and a settled home. Sally had a wisp of a body, as weightless appearing as an airborne leaf, and the energy of a spinning top. Her hair was blond and fine and silky, and she had a delightful squeal and laugh. I soon learned that underneath Sally's silly activity was a serious piece of talent — she was an artist with pen and ink and paints, something she had been practicing since the age of four. Sally brightened up my life the way she added colors to her pictures. My years in Kansas City had seemed like a black-and-white sketch, and then in the nick of time, just as I was ending childhood, she entered and colored my new life with laughs and games. That memory picture has not faded, and neither has our friendship.

Sally and I lived one house apart from each other on a street filled with American Revolutionary history. Bennington's important part in the Revolution is marked by a statue of an oversized mountain cat, called The Catamount, just up the street from where Sally and I lived. The Catamount statue is on a narrow green near the spot where a tavern known by the same name once stood. The tavern is important to Revolutionary history because it is where The Green Mountain Boys, a rough and ready group of local musket-bearing men, plotted their battles. The Catamount sculpture is a female mountain lion in motion, like a lynx or a leopard, with its teeth bared (no pussycat) on top of a huge piece of gray Vermont granite. The statue towers above a tall person and requires at least one pair of clasped hands to make a step for a young climber's foot to get on top of the granite. It was a challenge for Sally and me to mount The Catamount in broad daylight without some resident historian coming along and reprimanding us for what would best be described as "desacralizing our village god." I was impressed that people thought the fierce-looking mountain lion needed protection from a wispy little blond girl and her skinny newcomer friend.

"Are there really big cats like this around?" I asked Sally as we left The Catamount after we were told to climb down. We were scouting for another place to play.

"Oh, yes, in the mountain behind our houses." Sally had snatched a long blade of grass to blow through while we exchanged this important information.

"Do they ever come down here?" I suddenly became serious about our conversation.

"Not yet," she said, blew a long shrill whistle through her piece of grass, and then laughed.

"Are they green?" I asked in earnest.

"Green? You mean the grass? Are you color-blind?" She looked astonished, and then she tilted her head, put the blade of grass right up between her eyes, and crossed them to inspect it closely. I had to laugh at Sally's silly face.

"No, the mountain cats," I said pointing back toward The Catamount. "That one's green." It was green, of course, because it was aged bronze.

"Oh, Peggy," Sally said. "You've made a funny."

I had not meant to make a funny. The huge, blue-green Catamount was a powerful-looking prowler on our street and, although it appeared as still as a sphinx, I intended to know everything I could about the real thing. I had a long list of things to learn about my new life, and I determined right away that mountain lions should be number one.

☐

I completed the eighth grade of elementary school in Bennington, and my parents assumed that I would go away to boarding school. But I balked about the prospect like a bronco in place.

"No," I said firmly. "I've finally got two parents and lots of new friends. I've got a home. I'm staying put and going to public high school."

The bargain I made with my stepmother was not only fair but considerably in my favor. She insisted on compensating for what she thought I would lose academically and put me on a summer reading program of her own design. I read "good books" every afternoon while lounging on a wicker chaise on the downstairs screened-in porch overlooking the garden and beyond to the side of the mountain. She set me up with a local retired teacher to study *David Copperfield*, and she encouraged me to continue with my music lessons. My stepmother, it turns out, was my teacher for "applied aesthetics."

She also let me have my own kitten, which was hard on her old cat. I think my growing kitten wore the tired mouser out because one day it just lay down and died underneath the porch. My kitten, unfortunately, became pregnant before she was full-grown; but at least this time I knew the condition when I saw it.

"You've just become a teen-ager," I scolded my cat as one who knew. "And you're going to have to raise a family before you've had any fun yourself."

My cat seemed to understand that she was in over her head because when it came time for her to birth she stuck to me like sticky tape. I went to the neighbors across the street to get a cardboard box and rags for her birthing bed, and she waddled right beside me. I kept thinking that it was my second chance at a kitten birth and about how much I wanted this litter to live. They did, and the tiny ratlike creatures turned into infant kittens when they dried off. I was so proud of my little mother cat, and she was quite relieved.

I had several jobs as a teen-ager, but my favorite one was working for a family of my stepmother's relatives in the summers. They had a cottage on a Maine island, where I took care of their four children and did domestic work. On my time off, I had a wonderful time with a bunch of friends my age.

One summer, when I returned home, my cat was gone. I could not get answers to my questions as to her whereabouts. Had she been killed? Run over by a car? Did she run away? The latter was implied. I felt responsible for her fate because I had left her for the summer. Finally, after a few weeks of my bemoaning the loss, my stepmother confessed that while I was gone they had given my cat to the farmer who lived up on the mountain beside our house. She agreed to find out if the cat was still there and drive me up the mountain to retrieve her.

It was a warm September afternoon as we drove up a dusty, bumpy road to the mountain farm. The leaves had just begun to turn so the view was all aglow with variegated colors: green with yellow, green with red or orange, and green with cinnamon. I was aglow myself with anticipation about reuniting with my cat.

The farm was at the top of the small mountain in a hollow with yellowed fields circled by the turning trees. I had been to the farm several times before because it was just beyond my step- mother's mountain cabin and we sometimes bought homemade butter from the farmer's wife. I had always imagined that the storybook girl Heidi lived in a world like the mountain farm landscape.

My cat was nowhere to be found, the farmer told us.

"I'm sorry, it was here yesterday when you called," he apolo- gized while looking at my stepmother and avoiding me. "It plumb disappeared this morning."

I did not believe him or my stepmother. It was a trick, I thought. I was sure they were in cahoots. I think the farmer knew that because he began talking fast about what he thought might have happened.

"We've got a dozen cats around our farm, but they're all wild. Barn cats, you understand. Yours," he said as he finally looked directly at me, "is domesticated and just didn't fit in with the others. We couldn't let it in the house if we wouldn't let the others in. It was a nice cat. I'm sorry."

"Where would it go then?" I asked as I looked around and saw only the forest's edge and the blue sky.

"Into the woods. They'll do that," he concluded.

I was not foolish about the mountain's woods. I knew they were home to wild animals and how the wild things fed. My cat would be supper for some beast.

I worried every day that fall about what had happened to my cat. My worst fear, the nightmare variety, was that a mountain cat had snared her. I could hear her screeching in my imagination. I visualized mountain cats as looking like the bronze Catamount up the street: as big as tigers, green, and fierce. There were no real big green cats in the mountains behind our house, or anywhere; I knew that; but I still had an irrational fear that a huge green cat had eaten my little lost cat.

In reality, however, nature played a more important role than my shadowy misgivings as I worried about my cat's fate. As long as the snow had not settled on the ground for winter, I had hope for her return.

Two days before Christmas, as I was wrapping presents, snowflakes filled the air and within minutes all the outside world was white. Only then did I concede that the phantom catamount had beaten out Mother Nature.

At that very moment, when I had given up all hope, I heard a pathetic meow from the porch where I had read in the summertime. I rushed to what I thought was probably a stray (any cat would do) and found my own poor scraggly, skinny cat lying exhausted by the door. I could not believe it, of course. I had heard of miracles, but I never expected one to come to me. She had crossed a mountain, seen three full moons from a forest's vantage point, and escaped all the wild beasts between the farm and her destination . . . to return to me.

She fattened up quickly with lots of sleep and food and stayed with us until I left for college a few years afterward. The cat's return was as positive a force for me as my mother's removal and my grandmother's leaving had been negative. Mother Nature, I learned, has her ways.

A catamount did not get my cat, but it seized upon me permanently. It appears in my dreams, as unexpected as any wild beast surprises prey; but I tame its presence in the daytime when I remember that it is my messenger, not my predator. The catamount is a sign of my sense of self — and I find it in Vermont.

□ □ □ □

Pandora's Box

When I was sixteen, my mother was released from the mental hospital, due largely to Thorazine, a psychopharmacological "miracle drug" of the 1950s. Her sudden recovery stunned me like a blinding light. I had been hoping all those years that she would get well and come back to me, but when she was well, there was no place for her in my life. Her release opened up for me a kind of Pandora's box filled with tension and anxieties and demons and, later I discovered, hope.

There was a brief flurry of talk about her release. For the first time, I heard a name for her illness: a diagnostic label that included dangerous people, was usually incurable, and for which, therefore, being put away was a justifiable first choice of treatment. My father claimed my mother suddenly got well because her mother had died the year before; and my mother's family, I learned from my father's and stepmother's conversations, claimed it was because my father had remarried. I then understood that my father's family and my mother's family had been warring relentlessly for years over the cause of my mother's incarceration. Now, they were fighting over the reasons for her release. As soon as I sought to see my mother, I left behind ten years of innocence and ignorance and stepped right into my family's opened Pandora's box.

My mother had gone to live with her brother in their home-town on the other side of the Green Mountains. In order to visit her, I had to have someone drive me over the mountains to my uncle's home. The first trip was excruciatingly difficult. I sat silently in the back seat, as my father drove and my stepmother accompa-nied him in the front, and worried that I was hurting one parent at the expense of seeing or living with the other. The internal pressure mounted, and we stopped along a mountain pass so I could throw up. Then I was dropped off for the afternoon at my mother's temporary home.

I asked my father if he was going to get out and say hello to my mother, and he replied a sure no. I mounted the few porch steps to greet this woman who looked thinner and hollower than the already thin woman I remembered. She had the same flushed cheeks and the very light blue eyes I remembered, and she felt warm to kiss and she smelled the same.

My memory of the reunion with my mother is like a film of our earlier separation in reverse. The memory-film was taken at our home in 1947 when I was seven, the day we left her to go to my grandparents' Vermont farm and two weeks before blackberry season when she would be taken away. When the film is played backward, Dad drives into a driveway instead of out, and I get out of the car instead of in. My mother is standing at a house's side door when I go to greet her at age sixteen, just as she was standing at our home's side door when we left her and she shouted to me, "You'll be back." It is as if in order for me to return to her the memory-moving picture must be rewound. My memory of that day stops at the door.

Subsequent visits are clearer in my memory. My mother and I would rendezvous in a restaurant or in a parked car, and we worked hard at becoming reacquainted. It was tough sledding because I was a full-fledged adolescent and she was high-strung and somewhat disconnected.

Eventually, my mother moved into her own little rented room and worked as a licensed practical nurse in a nursing home. On one of my visits, she invited me to her room which she was proud to call her home. It was a very small upstairs room with one window and no bath or kitchen, yet it was quite homey because she had filled it with her handiwork projects. My mother had a sewing machine set up, and her room was filled with piles of neatly organized materials in a myriad of colors, half-finished quilts, yarns and sweaters she was making up, crochet hooks and balls of string, needlepoint, and tablecloths and napkins she was cross-stitching. That half hour with my mother was the closest time we ever had together when she was rational and I was not her baby: We were two females fingering through material as if we were trying to sort through the swatches and remnants of our torn relationship to no avail. We were so close, yet so far apart — so little time to last a lifetime.

She caught me up on a few missing pieces of my early life and personality that only a mother might notice.

"You were a sociable little being from the beginning," she told me one cold, snow-driven afternoon as we sat in the car on her town's main street. "Always reaching toward people with your hands and smiling. You'd make a good social worker if that's what you want to do."

My mother never commented on my father nor on my care, perhaps because she knew there was no way to recover her place in my life. Besides, she was busy struggling for her own survival, and I seemed healthy enough. We wrote to each other occasionally, but when I went to the Midwest for college, our letters dwindled to one or two a year. Then the little passage we had between us suddenly shut up as if an unexpected breeze had slammed an unstopped door. I was in my twenties before I sought her out again in earnest, and by then it was too late because she had stopped taking the Thorazine and staying in one place. My mother lost touch with reality and with people who knew and loved her, and within a few years she landed back in the hospital.

I had always listened quietly to whatever information I could gather about my mother, but it was scant. If I asked about her, which I rarely did, the replies were spartan. I never saw her family, and my father and his family either bit their tongues to keep from saying what they thought, or they hinted that her illness began before Dad had married her. Whatever information came my way came in code. I knew only that all my relatives were in a kind of perpetual cold war about my mother as if they were keeping in step with the long, political Cold War after World War II.

It was not until the 1980s, when I was in my forties and about the age my mother had been when she broke down, that I understood her illness was related to World War II and matters of the soul. She entered a personal crisis at the same time the war was at its peak. First, her hormones had probably kicked in with something new. Then, her sister and brother-in-law died two days apart and left three children, one of whom came to live with us. Dad had enlisted in the Army, so he moved my mother and her three charges to his hometown in Vermont, which was an isolating and sometimes hostile place for her. Then her father died. Then we moved again. It was her fifth house in the five years since she had given birth to me. My mother was a perfectionist. She must have been exhausted trying to prop up a fallen family and settle in new homes. At any rate, her spirit broke.

The mental health treatments at the time my mother was institutionalized were really tortures in disguise. Plus, as studies of personal crisis in mental hospitals have shown, patients in time of war do not respond favorably to treatment: Society in general is dominated by hostility, hatred, and military standards. My mother was an ordinary human being who might have gotten well if there had been no war. She never fought with military weapons or on any front, but I nonetheless came to see her as a prisoner of war in her mental illness: She spent forty years of confinement in a private hell that began around the same time as the Cold War.

□

My first appreciation of what World War II had done to ordinary people's lives came when I visited Norway in 1960. I was a twenty-year-old university student, impressionable, seeking independence, and working out the unresolved tension between my father and my mother. I was still suffering from our family's Pandora's box. I had had my first petit mal seizure two years earlier and begun a twenty-year treatment for the condition with prescription drugs, which masked the underlying anxieties. The short visit to Norway, although I did not know it at the time, planted the seeds that would help me reckon with my anxieties later on and gave me an understanding that my mother's mental illness was related more to the human soul than the mysterious brain.

My father and stepmother and I took a steamer trip in June up and back down the coast of Norway. The steamer was the mail boat, which took on a dozen cabin passengers as tourists for the entire trip, provided us with a tour guide, and stopped at every port to pick up and drop off Norwegian passengers whose only transportation between villages was this boat.

Emotionally, I was working on my own parents' divorce and their private cold war. Even the Norwegian mountains between villages reminded me of the Vermont mountains that geographically divided my parents, who were completely incommunicado.

The crew and tour guide invited me to join them for a glass of aquavit after dinner each evening. The guide translated for me the crews' stories about the war, the Resistance, and how the Nazis tried to break the Norwegian people's spirit by bombing the churches in every village. When we pulled into ports, I could see that the villagers were either rebuilding their churches or building them anew.

Suddenly a woman appeared on board who threw the crew and passengers into a state of shock. One night, we had docked in Trondheim, the most northern of Norway's major cities, and the next morning this woman showed up for breakfast in the cabin passengers' dining room. She was very tall, handsome and blond, and she was anything but welcome. I learned that was because she was German. She was completely ostracized for the whole trip as if she had leprosy. No one, not even the waiters, spoke to her. A kind of cold war in miniature had begun.

My stepmother said the hostilities toward the woman were unwarranted because she was a Bavarian German, and Bavarians had not wanted the war. But that did not matter to anyone else: The Bavarian was a pariah and a social prisoner on board that ship for an entire week.

The dynamic was painfully familiar to me. I watched the Bavarian being shut off as if I were watching my mother being ostracized because of her mental illness. The woman was about my mother's age. My sympathetic staring and my youth must have prompted her to speak to me one day when we were alone in a passageway. She said her reason for being on the ship was to view the midnight sun and asked if I would join her that evening to see it.

My memory of the night I watched the midnight sun with the Bavarian is like a fairytale of spending a short time alone with my mother. The sun that far north never sets in June, and in the well-lit midnight the dark ocean waters lifted various reflected colors on the crests of its waves. The fairytale even has my father taking a sleeping potion so I could be independent of one parent to work out a relationship with the other: He had miscalculated the effects of aquavit, gone to bed early, and slept until late the next day.

The Bavarian and I sat alone on the forward deck as the ship plowed due north, and we watched the great orange ball of sun dip below the horizon. Then, almost immediately, it reappeared. The setting and rising of the sun was so short a time for the passing of a day; so close appearing, yet so far away. In my memory, that fleeting time between two days feels like the few precious moments I had shared with my mother in her little room as we fingered through her handiwork materials.

My fairytale memory includes another image. The ship's prow kept bowing from the waves as if it were nodding at the sun to sight its position without celestial directions — a navigational occurrence called "dead reckoning." I was dead reckoning emotionally at age twenty, finding my way without my mother with imprints from early childhood and from the innate.

I look back on the Bavarian woman's brief appearance in my life as if she were my emotional guide for the trip. She had suddenly appeared on shipboard, and she spoke only with me. I had a chance to be company for someone as I hoped someone was being for my mother. The Bavarian and I shared a short but special time, and I gained some outward images of inward matters I was working out. Plus, she had boarded in Trondheim and would disembark there, too, where I would follow her down the gangplank to an experience that shaped my life.

□

My rendezvous with the Bavarian produced an outcry from the crew the next evening. They were sure she had filled my head with lies about the war. I assured them she had not and said she was disembarking in Trondheim soon anyway. Because they wanted to be sure I heard the truth about the war, they had arranged for me to get off in Trondheim, too, for the day. I was to meet someone they were sure would help me understand why they had ostracized the German woman.

The tour guide had a good friend in Trondheim whom he telegraphed to ask if she would host me when we arrived in port. This remarkable woman was trying to revive the Norwegian spirit through folk dances, and the tour guide was a member of her troupe.

As the steamer pulled into the dock at Trondheim, I looked for an old woman in native costume. The woman who met me was neither old nor costumed. My new Norwegian friend was in her late twenties, with dark hair and rosy cheeks, and she was very friendly.

"I'm taking you to the highest point overlooking the harbor," she said in perfect English. Before I knew it, we had climbed a good-sized hill and were on the promised precipice in ten minutes. We laughed like old friends as the woman unpacked our lunch and produced a crusty bread, sardines, and fruit.

"I like to come here because it is so beautiful, but also because the war is over," she said. "This is one of the strategic places where the enemy mounted their artillery."

I thought she was going to tell me about her revival of the Norwegian folk dances and songs, or about the war or the pagan god Thor; instead, she asked me about my life and studies and about America. I finally surmised that the troupe was not her work but something she volunteered to do in between her family responsibilities and her job—something in her blood. Since I was not Norwegian and did not need "reviving," telling me about the folkways would be a waste of time. However, I felt she had something in store for me.

We did not linger after lunch. My friend said I must see a very special place before she went back to work, so we hurried down the little mountain to a junction in the paths where we turned to walk up another steep hill.

"Now, you will see our cathedral," she said as if that were the reason I had come to Norway.

I expected the cathedral would be in rubble or under reconstruction, but as we rounded a bend of poplars it appeared intact: a charcoal gray, twin-towered, small Gothic cathedral looking like an apparition in the green park the way the Norwegian mountains loom in the fog along a fjord. It was the first cathedral I had ever seen.

On the walk up the hill my friend told me the history of what I was about to see.

"Trondheim was called Nidaros long ago, so this is the Nidaros Cathedral. It was built here because of Norway's King Olav, our great saint. Saint Olav was killed in battle and buried on this site, and immediately a spring of healing waters sprang up around him. Then a church was built around the healing waters and later the cathedral."

We were both slightly out of breath. As we reached the doors of the cathedral, my friend put our short hike in perspective.

"By the fourteenth century this had become a great shrine, and thousands of people from all over Northern Europe made their religious pilgrimages here. Just think of how far they walked."

She led the way into the cathedral purposefully. It was dark and cold, but up above a warm light radiated through narrow lancet windows. The stained-glass rose window at the west end, which I stretched my neck to look up at, was very large but dark. The woman said that under the right conditions, when the sun was at a good angle, the window looked like a huge full moon and filled the dark cathedral with light. I followed her through the nave to the choir where she stopped.

"When I was a little girl, I played the violin," she said as she looked around the choir. "Everyone in our family played some instrument, and we played together a lot. But we stopped making our music when Norway was occupied."

She had focused on a stone railing about forty feet above us. Built into the wall all around the choir, it looked like an architectural facade.

"That is a very narrow balcony," she said as she pointed to the railing. "Just wide enough for a child to lie down on her side. I know because I did it once." Then she turned and pointed to the crossing between the transept and the nave just a few steps below us. "During the Nazi occupation, chamber music was played here once a week. Right here," she emphasized by repeatedly pointing toward the crossing. Then she slowly swung her arm in an arc in front of her to indicate the cathedral seats. "And the audience was filled with Germans."

I looked at the crossing and tried to imagine what the musicians looked like. Were they in uniform, playing violins and flutes and piccolos? Did the music touch their souls? Were the musicians conscripted Norwegians? I imagined the cathedral filled with German military men. Then I asked her if Norwegians came to hear the music.

"Oh, no, we weren't allowed. Of course, people would not have wanted to be anywhere near them, anyway." Then she took me gently by my elbow and spoke quite intimately. "But this is what I want to tell you. This is why I brought you here. My brother and I once heard music in this very place. It was at one of their weekly Nazi concerts. Our parents did not know we were going to do what we did. If they had, they would have stopped us because if we'd been caught, we might be dead."

She became quite animated as she recalled the experience.

"Very late at night, the night before the concert, my brother and I sneaked into the cathedral. We went up to the balcony and spent the night." As she pointed to the side where they had slept, she looked disbelieving. "And we stayed completely still all through the next day while they were setting up for the concert. Never moved or talked."

I guessed that she must have been about twelve years old at the time, and I could still remember what it felt like to be that age.

"That evening we heard what we had come for, the first music we had heard in years. It was beautiful! We stayed down low on the balcony floor, all cramped up throughout that night, and sneaked out in the early morning hours."

I knew I had heard an important story from someone close to my generation, and it affected me more than the words of the ship's crew. She and her brother had risked their lives and their parents' lives to satisfy their souls with music in the great Norwegian shrine. And those Nazis were entertaining themselves on Norway's most sacred ground, striking to demoralize, the way they had bombed the village churches.

The crew's and tour guide's plan to educate me about the war had worked. But I also learned about the human spirit from my Norwegian friend who hid in balconies. I have a momentary reprieve from my anxieties when I imagine her as I never saw her: dressed in native costume with one hand positioned on her waist and the other arm through her partner's — dancing, dancing around again and again on top of Norway's healing waters in the Nidaros Cathedral. The church is packed with Norwegians, and children are clapping from the balconies to cheer her on.

I know the fantasy of the dancing woman is really for my mother: my wish for her that her spirit had not been crushed by war and darkness. People had believed for centuries that the Nidaros shrine had healing power, and the sacred place had withstood the presence of a great evil. Perhaps I thought there could be some miracle for my mother the way the miracle drug Thorazine had seemed to promise that she would be permanently restored.

I also had a great fear that I would someday succumb to mental illness, and I needed hope that my spirit would not be broken. The Norwegian woman's story gave me that hope as surely as my mother's release from the mental hospital had opened a whole Pandora's box of anxieties for me.

The Greek myth about Pandora and her box is a story I now understand through my own experiences. Pandora was the first woman in Greek myths, and when she married, she took with her as a dowry a vase — which is what we refer to as Pandora's box. She was persuaded to open the vessel, and out flew evil spirits until all that was left inside, that which did not fly away, was hope. The Greek story does not mean to me what tradition has come to say about it: that woman is the one who brings evil to the world. Man does not bring it either. Evil, I believe, is just here without gender or nationality or race. No, the story means to me that at the bottom of the human spirit is the gift of hope. I learned that from a woman of my generation — a Norwegian folk dancer who restored human spirits, including mine.

III.

Reckoning

A Time to Cast Away, A Time to Keep

CHAPTER 13

□ □ □ □

The Barn

When I was thirty-six, my father's sister, Aunt Cynie, whose daughters had treated me like their sister when we were young, gave me an invaluable and intangible treasure that was disguised as a dirty job. My husband and our two young children and I were visiting the ancestral Vermont village where my grandparents had poured country medicine into me when I was seven. Our visits to the village in years past had been to see Gramma, but even they were few and far between because we lived so far away: in the Midwest, my husband's home territory, and then in eastern Maine. But, after Gramma died, I made an effort to see Aunt Cynie whenever possible as if she were my familial touchstone.

She and Uncle Andy lived next door to the house my parents had bought during World War II as a home for my mother, her orphaned niece, my brother, and me while Dad was serving in the Army. Thirty years later, I was sitting in the bay window of Aunt Cynie's kitchen, looking at the small red barn that belonged to our old house, and thinking that it was a classic architectural archetype of Vermont. The old, narrow, two-story building has white-paned windows, red-stained double doors on the first floor, and a small white door on the second floor tucked beneath the eaves above the barn entrance. It was through that white door — the hayloft aperture — that I was to discover secrets that had been buried for thirty years.

"You'd better come some weekend and clean out your father's barn," my aunt advised me.

"It's not Daddy's barn," I corrected her. "Why, he sold the house and barn almost twenty years ago. I've got no connections to it."

"Well, yes, you do," Aunt Cynie replied kindly. "I think the hayloft is chock right full with your mother's things, and you should see them. Besides, the people who own your old place are good neighbors, and I'd like to keep it that way. They need to be rid of the stuff, and they've been kind not to throw it out before now. I'm sure they'd like the space themselves," she added so I would understand that cleaning out the barn was the decent thing to do.

I looked out her kitchen window at the old red barn in disbelief that my family's things (if there really were any that I did not know about or had not seen) were in someone else's barn. Several rows of clothesline were strung from the side of the barn to weathered posts where my mother's garden once stood. The maple tree was still there. A lower branch that once held my swing was now too high for such frivolity.

My best memories of my mother are tied up in that space. She tended her Victory Garden, picking beans and thinning carrots, while I traveled through the air on the swing. I pretended I could see my father doing "Army work" when I reached the peak of swing and looked over the rock-studded green pasture rolling down behind the barn.

"Why didn't Daddy ever clean it out?" I asked Aunt Cynie while she set the table and I kept rocking in the chair beside the window.

"I don't know, honey," she answered. "I've been wondering myself. But no matter. It's your doing now."

My mother was alive but, besides being physically and mentally incapable of doing the job, she would never be included in the invitation due to the permanent family rift. My father by this time had been diminished by arterial diseases. There was no asking him to clean out the mess, and, besides, he might have put it there intending it to rest. Dad, who was tight-lipped about family history anyway, had never told me about the hidden family treasure.

Apparently, I thought while gazing at the barn, two things had happened simultaneously, and disturbing one might breach the other: Our family possessions were stored at the same time my mother was put away. Were the goods in the barn to be forgotten along with my mother? Would it be too painful a memory to look at what was lost? Or did preserving the barn's contents keep the good memories alive? I feared that if the red barn secret was my father's way of sealing good memories, my emptying it might break the spell.

□

My husband, our children, and I returned to Vermont six months after Aunt Cynie asked me to clean out the barn. I knew as little about its contents as I knew then about my mother's mental breakdown — and I had no idea as to what good could be left from either disarray. I thought the household spoils had been divided up. My husband and I had lamps and chairs and dressers from my family all through our house and my mother's quilts upon our beds. I had used my mother's portable black sewing machine for twenty years. My father's living room still held the books and the oil seascape painting that had hung over a sofa when we lived with my mother, and over every sofa afterward. I had a few pewter bowls for entertaining in style and some costume jewelry I never wore but looked at periodically. There could not be any more family treasure in that barn, I thought as we approached Aunt Cynie's.

The next day was perfect for cleaning out the barn. It was a clear, bright, windless October morning. The red and orange leaves were on the ground, but the golden oaks and the crimson maples still held their colors. The pastures and lawns were yellowing, and the evergreens outlined the woods.

Aunt Cynie's family stood by to help, as curious as I was about the contents. There was Mary, my favorite cousin; her brother Joe, a strong quiet man who had not even been born when I lived in the village; Uncle Andy, a quiet Frenchman with sharp brown eyes who was "foreman" on the day's job; and Aunt Cynie, who calculated from her kitchen window as to when we should be fed. And there was my husband, George, who had muscle enough from his Midwest farm boyhood to lug what we would haul out but who had no liking for the job.

"I've heard the old Vermont joke," George said without smiling, "about the couple who've been married for fifty years, and he tells his wife it was all he could do to keep from telling her that he loved her. We don't store up our feelings like that in the Midwest. This barn business is all Yankee nonsense to me."

Uncle Andy borrowed the neighbors' key to the padlock on their barn door and opened the double entrance for our anxious and curious little group. The old barn had a one-horse stall and a smell of wood shavings. There were farming tools stacked along a wall, but Uncle Andy said they were not ours.

"Your things are in the hayloft, Harriet," he said as he reached for a trapdoor above the stairs. "I've got no idea what's there. I haven't been up here since your father sold it."

We all followed Uncle Andy into the pitch black attic. He picked his way through boxes to the small outside hayloft door and tugged to open it. A perpendicular shaft of yellow light crossed the dust-filled air and lit enough so we could see it was not treasure to be uncovered but only a mess to be cleaned up. Magazines with mouse-eaten covers lay across the floor like a lumpy carpet, and piles of folders lurched like overturned radiators. There were empty cardboard and wooden boxes with their contents strewn from eave to eave, and children's playthings lying atop kitchen utensils next to rags that were once clothes.

"It's not the way I remember it," Uncle Andy exclaimed as he removed his dark green workman's cap and scratched his head.

"Kids must of gotten into it. Just sorting out could be a full day's job. How d'you want to go about it, Harriet?"

I suddenly felt weak. Our eyes had adapted to the darkness, yet I could not recognize a thing.

"Why clean up a mess that isn't mine?" I answered with a question.

"It's yours, all right," Joe said as he held up a browned manila envelope to the shaft of light. "This is addressed to your father. So's this pile," he pointed to an accordion of paper.

"And these are government publications from his job in the 1930s," Mary said from her kneeling position beneath an eave.

"Magazines by the truckload," George said caustically. "Ten thousand *Reader's Digest*s and *Saturday Evening Post*s, it seems. Everything published in his time, I guess."

If there was to be any joy in the job, it was the anticipation of finding something of my mother's. And we were wading through my father's papers. Inertia just set in for me. The decay was overpowering, and it had me in its grip. I could not speak, much less move, until George began pitching things.

"It all goes," he said as he flung an armload of magazines out of the hayloft door. "Let's just get this stuff out of here. I don't know how we're going to get rid of it once it's on the ground, but we've got to start somewhere."

The cleanup began as if we were emptying the loft of hay for a hungry herd below. The four of them worked feverishly but quietly, either throwing trash out or picking up below, while I stood in the center of the attic and surveyed what they uncovered. Uncle Andy worked out a scheme for disposing of the paper rubbish: They lugged it by hand and wheeled it by barrow to Uncle Andy's backyard and burned it in his trash barrel. The hauling and disposing took all day, and the great flame shot upward until early evening. It was cathartic work.

I stayed in the barn loft all day, sorting and deciding, while the others hauled and burned outdoors. Although I never saw the fire until I was finished with my job just before suppertime, I could envision the burning place from my childhood memories. It was on the edge of a crag overlooking the pasture where we romped as children and where I crossed with Grampa when he went to clean out the springhouse. On a summer's evening, when the breeze had died down to nothing, Uncle Andy would burn the week's trash until the barrel full was reduced to ash. Eight or ten of us, all cousins old enough to play outside until dark, would make a racket of wild gestures and unlikely noises around Uncle Andy's work like dancing primitives beside a funeral pyre.

"Swish and crackle." I heard the distant flames, like background music, while I worked quietly and alone in the upstairs of our old barn.

□

My mother's things were beneath the paper debris and overturned cartons of toys. They were packed neatly in boxes and often tied with string. Some boxes were marked. It was like my mother to keep such order, except I do not think she intended anything for storage. There had been only two weeks between the day we left my mother and her incarceration. Perhaps she busied herself with tidy packings during that time, expecting to move; but I doubt she was preparing for anything or anyone to be put away permanently. Seeing her hand in packing was a painful reminder of how lonely and bewildered she must have been while I, her little girl, was being settled in someone else's home.

The order of my mother's things was a great contrast to the disorder covering it. It was as if my father and my brother and I had gone berserk with our possessions because she had unhinged internally. There was no sense or comfort in either the order or the chaos.

The pieces of a wooden lawn bowling set were strewn atop a stretch of Lincoln Logs with canvas sling chairs and seats thrown in between. A freestanding baby's swing without the seat was crumpled on top of children's building blocks. My dollhouse was buried in the mess with its roof ten feet away. I found the dollhouse furniture in all parts of the hayloft throughout the day. It looked like a tornado had hit my little home. A miniature red couch and chair were nestled by a bed between two packing boxes, and I found an old-fashioned sink on legs in a corner, along with the tiny fireplace with logs and flames painted on a cardboard insert. I picked up pieces of my imaginary home as if I could straighten in one decorative mood what had blown apart thirty years before.

Fingering familiar childhood things took me back in time. I wondered how I could have forgotten my favorite toys. There was no question: They were mine. Alone in the warm barn while my family was busy burning trash, I had precious time to contemplate my mother's boxes before I opened them. Maybe archaeologists have that same moment when they open up a sealed tomb and wonder what their prying will unleash.

I could not leave the boxes in someone else's barn, and I could not lug them four hundred miles to my home. They had to be unsealed.

The first cardboard box contained a half dozen pairs of women's shoes. I tried one on, of course. It was a full size bigger than my foot. My mother was tall. All the shoes were well-kept, fashionable high heels from the 1940s — sling-backed and in pastel colors; but there was no worth in saving them.

There was a small carton of desk-drawer items that told a short story of the day they were packed: paper clips, three-cent stamps, blank paper and envelopes for correspondence, pens from my father's company, a few photographs of my brother and his playmates and one of me, letters dated August 1947, and a small box of calling cards with my mother's married name.

Some cartons contained smaller boxes, such as Fanny Farmer candy boxes or flowered boxes for gloves. Each was neatly packed. One had four compacts: little silver or tapestry-covered containers for powder and a mirror. Another had costume jewelry: plastic rings and stone-studded metal bracelets. And another box held a tortoiseshell-framed mirror and a matching comb. My mother was pretty and well-groomed. She had high cheekbones, very light blue eyes, and a long regal nose. Her hair was dark brown, and she wore it in a pompadour. I flashed the hand mirror's light against the rafters and the dark corners and remembered my mother as I had seen her when I was a child.

"No," I answered someone's question from below about trash. "I've got nothing for you now. And there must be a dozen more boxes to go through. Give me time!"

A grape purple-painted blanket chest with pastel green trim stood against the eave. They were unusual colors, but I had seen the combination before. It was the basis for a patchwork quilt on a bed at home. My mother must have worked carefully with paint and cloth to decorate some room. She majored in home economics and taught the course in high school before she married, and she had continued to apply her knowledge in her home.

The chest contained my mother's memories. There were several albums of photographs and carefully wrapped envelopes of negatives. There were enough packages of black photo corners to paste up another album. My mother was an amateur photographer who, true to the hobbyist's trait, rarely appeared in pictures because she was always taking them. She caught her college friends in antics on a Ford running board or posed them in a lineup of flappers, wearing raccoon coats or sailor suits or cloches and long strings of beads. There were portraits of large family gatherings, either her clan or Dad's, but my mother is rarely shown, as if the pictures were photographic premonitions that she would disappear from our family life. My favorite picture is one of my mother readying her camera to take a photo of the person who shot her. She is wearing a light-colored, belted dress with short sleeves and shoulder pads, shading the projected lens of her collapsible camera, laughing and looking straight at the other photographer.

The blanket chest also held several stacks of letters tied in kitchen twine with bows. There were two sizes of bundles. One was square, a stack of lady's stationery and envelopes, and the other was rectangular, a gentleman's. They were, of course, my mother's letters to my father and his to her. My heart jumped. Perhaps this was their correspondence during the war and just before my mother's breakdown. Perhaps the letters would tell me what went wrong and why. I felt like the archaeologist at a tomb's unopened door for the second time that day. Should I untie a bundle?

Curiosity was a stronger urge than propriety. I found the letters were not domestic history; they were letters of the heart. Two hundred envelopes with folded pages about love, where to meet, and when to meet again. They were dated in the late 1920s, and all had New England postmarks and penmanship I recognized. I sat cross-legged in front of the hayloft door to catch the full light of that October afternoon, scanned love letters that had been written fifty years before, and felt as close to family treasure as I will ever need to be. I retied the bundles and put them in the pile to take home.

Several boxes contained clothes. The woolen goods were folded neatly and peppered with moth holes. The cottons were pressed but stained from spring moisture in the cardboard boxes. I saved two musty dresses to launder and hang among my stored dresses at home, reminders of my mother's height and shape — a tall, thin woman with proud carriage like a chieftain's. There were more boxes within boxes. One held baby blankets and one held layettes and bonnets. There were babies' socks (clean from baby being carried) and rattles that still rattled. I was as far back in my personal history as I could go.

There was a silver-colored suit box among the clothes. Tissue paper surrounded something light in weight and color, and I fingered down until I found a piece of ivory satin with lace. I did not dare to unfold it in the dirty barn, but I guessed the satin was my mother's wedding dress. I had already found my father's wedding suit and a white linen man's suit with vest and knickers — costumes of the 1920s and memories before my time.

Of all my mother's memorabilia, the box that struck me the hardest held her sewing things. She was a master seamstress, and she designed clothes. Among my mother's few papers was an award for winning a national dress-design contest, so I knew she was an artist in her field.

The box held thread and buttons and seam binding in a myriad of colors. And, like my mother's other well-packed boxes, this one contained a small cardboard box within. It held her final project, and the project was not yet done: aqua silk material cut into pieces with the pattern still attached. The directions and the picture were in the box, and the aqua thread, seam binding, and zipper were placed neatly atop the cloth. There was a small red pincushion with pins and needles and a pair of scissors, as if she had packed everything she needed to make up the dress.

It was the sense of major interruption that unnerved me. I believe my mother intended to finish the project and wear it to some party, to go on living in her gracious manner, and to raise her children. She did not mean to go mad or to have her treasures stored in someone else's barn.

I held the evidence of intention that day—a woman's creative pursuit in aqua — and I understood her loss for the first time instead of just bemoaning mine.

☐

Aunt Cynie's dining table looked as if she were feeding supper to a crew who had just raised a barn instead of emptying one. White ironstone platters and blue willowware bowls held sliced maple sugar-cured ham, a roasted chicken, baked beans and green beans, coleslaw from their garden cabbage, scalloped potatoes with Cheddar cheese, corn relish and cucumber pickles, homemade rolls, and a choice of red and orange jams. Three pies sat on the sideboard with a pot of coffee.

"Two apple pies for the Vermonters," Aunt Cynie jokingly pointed out, "and the lemon meringue is for our Midwestern guest."

We filled our empty spots with good food and laughter. Not much was mentioned about the pathos of the day's find. I had settled silently what I would take home and what I could pick up in the spring. Besides, there was no room for dark remembrances because a half dozen children — my cousins' and ours — were giggling at the supper table the way Mary, Liz, and I had done when we were young.

"There's another hour of burning," Uncle Andy announced as he finished off his second piece of pie. "Just stack the dishes and come help me with the job."

It was nearly dark. A great orange flame shot out of the rusted trash barrel and threw streaks of light across the back pasture like spotlights on a stage. The flame's light picked out crevices, foxholes, and stony beds from rivulets that daylight had glossed over as if selecting details for a dream that consciousness had not seen. The children played and screeched like wild hyenas, and the neighbors' dog answered with a yapping of its own. We were completing unfinished business — tearing cartons, ripping magazines, and feeding the nighttime pasture light with the remnants of my first home.

Aunt Cynie and I unpacked my mother's wedding dress from the silver cardboard box that evening just before we went to bed. I was exhausted from the day and mystified and also somewhat angry that things I found to be family treasures had been stored up so secretively for thirty years. Aunt Cynie laid the unspoiled, ivory satin, slender frock across the guest room bed, and we both marveled at how thin my mother's figure had once been. The dress had a very slender bodice, a narrow waistband with a rosette of satin and lace at one side, and a slim drop of satin to the floor. As Aunt Cynie held up a lace sleeve to check for yellowing, my troubled emotions finally cleared.

"Thank you. You've given me a great gift," I said as I kissed her good-night. "I've finally reconnected with my past today."

"I'm glad you found so many of your mother's things in the barn," Aunt Cynie said while she gently folded the dress to fit into the silver box. "I'm sure it would please her if she knew."

□ □ □ □

A Ton of Honey

Treasures often look like trash. My mother's recipe collection rests inside a small, black, dried-up leather looseleaf notebook that I can easily cradle in one hand, and it is a wonder I never threw it out. Somehow, someone — my stepmother or my grandmother — had given me the little book when I was young and not interested in cooking, but I had moved it from place to place for almost thirty years before I really looked at it.

The pages are crinkly and yellowed, and a third of the 150 handwritten sheets have torn away from the spiral binding. The pages are out of order, and there are no detailed instructions beneath the lists of ingredients, but the book's value for me is not culinary, anyhow; it is a treasury of information about my mother which I harken back to in my search for self. It is written history, and combined with old photographs, it gives me a mental picture book of an era and a woman I hardly knew. I cannot call my mother and get domestic tips or genetic information; instead, I finger through the brittle pages and read between the lines.

My mother's maiden name is engraved across the cover in small gold letters. Someone may have given her the little black book when she graduated from college. The only dated entry is a page of menus for serving crowds: "Public supper to serve 150 persons" and "Health supper for 30 persons." The Health Supper calls for three salmon loaves, a quart of pimento sauce, mashed potatoes from a peck, banana and peanut salad, three loaves of bread, and coffee.

"Hmmm," is about all I can say.

I turn the page carefully and see menus for a Football Banquet and a Senior Luncheon, both dated 1928. "Yes," I say to myself, that is the year my mother graduated from the University of Vermont with a degree in home economics.

There is genealogy in the treasure, names of my mother's friends and mentors, and a picture of the pre-World War II way of life. I track this information through the names written below the recipes. It is often a relative's or a friend's name or a reference such as *American Cookery* or someone's hometown.

"Mother" is for my mother's mother, and "Mother H" is for her mother-in-law. My mother's aunts, sisters, and sisters-in-law are named beneath a few recipes. When Aunt Cynie, my father's sister, realized I had salvaged my mother's cookbook, she begged to borrow it.

"Oh my, that's worth a ton of honey," she said, clasping her hands just below her face as if she were preparing to pray. "I promise not to lose it. Your mother, my, could she ever cook."

"It's older than the hills," I said, doubting that she would really want it. "Very few instructions — just ingredients, often without measurements. Who'd know what to do?"

"Oh, I would," she smiled. "I measure by the eye anyway. Recipes were passed on in the kitchen in my day. We watched our mothers cook or cooked with them at our elbows, you know. We didn't read anything from some book. That's what makes this such a treasure," she said, holding the small, black, looseleaf book in both hands as if it were her prayer book.

The book has one reference to the person who must be my mother's namesake: Aunt Mattie's Pineapple Sherbet. Mattie is my mother's name and the sherbet recipe is the only evidence I have that she was named for a family member. Since I was named for my mother's favorite aunt, a Harriet, I speculated that my mother was named for someone her mother adored — a sister or an aunt. The speculation is like deciphering a "t" beside an ingredient in the recipes. Is it a teaspoon or a tablespoon? Was my mother's namesake an aunt or a great-aunt? There is no one at my elbow to guide me.

So much for genealogy.

□

Of the forty friends and mentors named beneath the recipes, I know only two personally. I have heard of a few others or seen them in my mother's photograph book. I figured out that her mentors are listed as "Mrs." and her friends by their first names — the former are older women and the latter, my mother's peers. The "missuses" are mothers of my mother's friends, a woman with whom she boarded when she was teaching school (Mrs. Fitz, short for Fitzpatrick — a compromise between mentor and friend?), two doctors' wives (one whose husband delivered me), and neighbors (one who tended me my first year). But most I cannot trace. The friends were my mother's childhood playmates, college chums, fellow teachers, and others I do not know. Two recipes come from men. Clark's Pull Taffy is from Uncle Clark, a smiling, laughing man who could make pulling taffy your favorite thing to do.

Sometimes when I read the names of the recipes in my mother's book, I pretend they were named after her because of how she looked and acted. She was funny, quick, very pretty, and she loved her college chums. But of all the recipes, the cake titles portray her best: Lightning, Eagle, Marble Sunshine, and College Fudge. One chocolate cake, with lots of sugar, shortening, and eggs in the recipe, has her red-penciled comment, "good but expensive."

"My, she was thrifty, too," Aunt Cynie said. "She could make a meal from nearly nothing on the shelves."

There are "no-sugar" cakes and "eggless" cakes. I look for "butterless" or something specifying margarine because I have only one "at my elbow" cooking memory of my mother. It was

World War II and I was four years old. I was learning how to color margarine, or she was keeping me from being underfoot. I wrestled with a chair to be at the right height to stir the white, lardlike substance in a bowl on the kitchen table.

"You put the color in," my mother said as she handed me a little opened packet. "I'll stir first. You sprinkle the magic, and together we'll make butter."

The "magic" was a paprika-colored powder. Red, veinlike streaks swirled in the white fat while my mother worked the wooden spoon one way and the bowl the other. When my turn came, I pounded the spoon up and down the way I had seen a butterchurn move. I was useless but it was fun, and the memory is worth a ton of honey.

The dessert names are titles from another time. Puddings are Snow, Peanut Butter, Indian, and Grapenut; English Plum, Coffee, Graham Cracker, and Callas. Callas? There is Rhubarb Tapioca and Apple Tapioca. The ices are a trip through memory lane of hand-churned ice cream and "automatic refrigerator" sherbets. The names evoke colors in the mind: Lemon, Chocolate, Vanilla, and Caramel; Pineapple, Cranberry, Fruit (your choice), and Martha's. Martha's? (Your choice. I choose a gold-colored sherbet because my matron of honor was a Martha, and she wore a gold dress in our wedding to match her honey-colored hair.)

There are breads and muffins and heavy cakes like Fruit Cake and Bangor Brownies, the latter rich with chocolate and perhaps with memories of a trip to Maine. There is Auntie Sweetland's Graham Nut Bread. Auntie Sweetland? Is that my mother's sense of humor? No, the lady's name appears again. But what a title for a bread! Auntie Sweetland is my mental heading for the section on desserts and breads.

The cookbook holds lots of secrets for making things that we now buy ready-made. Preserved and canned items include a wealth of pickle recipes like Winter Salad. There is Chili Sauce, Ketchup, Tomato Juice, and Green Tomato Marmalade (waste not, want not, I suppose); Raspberries, Corn, White Cherry Jam, and Marsh-

mallows. There are remedies for bronchitis and scabies and recipes for Cough Medicine and Hand Lotion.

My favorite preconsumer recipe is one for a French wine with
the source listed as the Mailman. Who was he? What other conversations did they have besides this one about wine? Had he been to
France and, if so, was it during a war? Did she hum the tune for
"How're You Gonna Keep Him Down on the Farm after He's Seen
Paree?" when she stirred the gallon of juice and water with three
pounds of sugar? "Put in keg," she wrote, "and keep filled with
water and a bit of sugar for several weeks." I imagine her humming
while she tends the keg and then running to meet the mail.

"Oh, I wish I'd hear from him." I can resurrect my mother's
voice when we lived without Dad during World War II. While he
served his country in uniform, she served our family by caring for
three children — her orphaned niece, my brother, and me — and
her Victory Garden.

Slipped between Tomato Mincemeat and Waffles I found my
mother's greatest domestic secret — newspaper clippings related
to her marriage. There was the engagement announcement, notice of a surprise shower, and a lengthy report on the wedding
ceremony and reception (pink and green motif, and chicken pot
pie for supper). I doubt that my mother could have separated
marriage from domestic management, good nutrition from raising
children, or frugality from survival. She was old-fashioned in intent
and modern in ability, so the little black book of recipes would
naturally include the reason for collecting them.

The last six inches of the yellowed clipping about my parents'
wedding include the names of out-of-town guests.

"There they are," I exclaim. "Half of those listed are in my
mother's cookbook as recipe donors. What a gift!"

☐

My mother was a real "domestic engineer," a woman who
took up homemaking as a serious profession. She broke down
about the same time home remedies and recipes from scratch went

out of vogue, and packaged shelf items and more convenient foods came in. My mother and her style of homemaking were both put by, so to speak; which is how, and perhaps why, her carefully compiled cookbook comes to be a last testament of sorts for her. It is proof, at least to me, that she intended to provide for her progeny.

Only one recipe sticks in my memory as something my mother cooked for me: Baked Tomato Rarebit. This simple dish predates pizza as a parent's answer to fill a child: "Place sliced bread on a greased baking pan, top each piece with a thin slice of club cheese, then top with sliced fresh tomatoes or drained canned tomatoes, and finally top with bacon. Bake for about thirty minutes and then brown in broiler." I used to treat our children to the bubbly red and yellow hot sandwich and fill myself up, too.

The reading of my mother's last testament is often lyrical.

I find Cousin Effie's Buns and Mrs. Fitz's Sauce; Aunt Ann's Cream Pie and Green Mountain Sauce. The sauce would be something from Vermont. It uses one and a half cups of maple syrup, one-half cup of vinegar, nutmeg, and one "t" of butter. How to cook it? It does not say. Spoon over what? Something that needs sweetening, I suppose.

Spatters on some pages make the ink spread out like finger-prints. Those recipes may be illegible, but my mother's mark is still there.

She wrote down a recipe that I can use to taste the ton of honey memory. It is marked "clever" by my mother. If I were adding to her book, I would mark it with a gold star. The recipe is for — you guessed it — Honey.

"Boil to heavy syrup: five pounds of sugar and three cups of water. Then add one 't' of powdered alum and boil two minutes. (Now comes the pretty part.) Let stand in syrup ten minutes: forty red clover blossoms, thirty white clover blossoms, and five pink roses. (I like knowing there are pink roses in the recipe. Don't you, too?) Strain, cool, and can."

Can you taste it?

In a lighter colored pen but in the same graceful script, my mother wrote below the honey recipe, "Be sure the flowers are not too old."

Treasure hunters often grasp at little things and call them clues. My mother's faded footnote is written proof to me that she used this recipe.

Sometimes when I need to have my mother "at my elbow," the homemade Honey recipe does provide. I do not imagine her stirring a boiling pot or standing in a syrup-vapored hot kitchen. Instead, I see her gathering her clover. It is early summer, bright and fresh, and my mother is a young woman as I remember her. She moves intently among the clover blossoms, bending and kneeling. Then she stands and stretches and puts one hand on her waist to massage a soreness in her lower back. She stares ahead to focus on thin air as if it held a message about the future. It is a brief moment, one when I can talk to her and pretend that she can hear.

In those elusive moments, when time does not matter or interfere, I mime a myriad of messages to my mother. Some are childish wishes for what I missed, and some are assurances that I made it to adulthood in one piece.

If I had found a recipe for alchemy, such as the medieval hunt to turn base metal into gold, I would not be any happier than I am with my mother's written domestic legacy. I hold the brittle, black leather treasure etched in gold and whisper to her, in that moment when I imagine her resting from picking clover, "Thank you, thank you, Mattie, for the inheritance. It's worth a ton of gold."

□ □ □ □

CHAPTER 15

Return to Country Medicine

"We'll eat when milking's done," my cousin Mary said when she greeted us at her kitchen door.

My husband and I and our two children had driven all day from our home in eastern Maine to visit Mary and her family on their dairy farm in western Vermont. We were tuckered out, but the sight of Mary's cheerful face revived us.

"I'm sure you're hungry," she apologized as we dragged into her well-lit, warm kitchen, "but on the farm dinner's served just once, and it's suited to the cows' schedule."

We knew what Mary meant — that her husband, Bill, was still out in the barn milking — but we laughed at the image of some seventy cows barreling into Mary's kitchen to be fed.

"Oh, Sweet Pea and Turkey, you are funny." Mary laughed as she called our daughter and son by the pet names she and Bill had for them. The children had hulked over as if they were cows, pulled out chairs from the table with their heads, and clumsily plopped into them. "Nope, I don't let any animals in my house — I mean *any* — except our dog. And people who act like animals can't come in either." She played along with their charade as she moved a pot of boiling vegetables off the stove.

This was our third or fourth visit to Mary's, and she and her family had made as many to be with us just in the past few years. We were making up for a host of lost time because Mary and I had not seen each other for over twenty years. Though Mary and her sister, Liz, had taken me on as their sister when I was living with our grandparents, we were in our early thirties and in the thick of raising our families when we met again, two years before we cleaned my family's things out of the barn. We had grown apart like branches on a tree, yet when we reconnected, we immediately understood that we had come from the same roots.

When Mary was six and I was seven, someone took a picture of us standing in front of the trunk of a big maple tree. I call the old black-and-white photograph our "bonding picture." Mary has light-colored hair and mine is dark. The only similar things about us are the shapes of our eyes and our hair styles — we both wore it parted in the middle and pulled straight back into barrettes. I am a full head taller than Mary and wearing new dungarees, which show my knees are bent, as if I am trying not to tower above her. My thumbs are awkwardly draped around the bottom button of my pea jacket. I have the beginning of a smile as if I am thinking about whether I should enjoy being photographed: the picture of ambivalence.

Mary, on the other hand, is looking at the camera with determination and no smile. She is standing straight without a doubt about how tall or short she should be, wearing wool pants and a wool sweater, and holding a doll firmly against her chest so it can be photographed, too. The doll is wearing a dress, and its legs stick straight forward because Mary is holding it so tightly. Its head and one arm are thrown sideways, and one can easily imagine it yelling, "Help!" The doll has become a standing joke between Mary and me because much of its hair is gone. Mary likes to say I probably pulled her dolly's hair and that is why she looks so mad.

Mary and I grew up very differently. She stayed in one place; I did not. She was raised in our ancestral village with three siblings and two parents who worked hard, kept a routine around her father's rotating eight-hour shifts at the paper mill, and kept a large garden. Although they did not farm for a living, their family patterns were much like our grandparents'. They lived frugally, valued education, and found a way for their children to go to college if they wanted to.

Mary had become a nurse. I had branched out quite differently.

"In a westerly direction," Mary says good-humoredly about what happened to me. I moved constantly. By the time I was thirty-four, when I reconnected with Mary, I had moved twenty-one times. I had been transient for five summers in my youth and for the four years of my higher education. I had gone to a university in the Midwest, married and had children, and then we moved to Maine. Five years after I returned east, Mary and I met at a classic juncture in a family's life: an elder's funeral. Gramma had died, and Mary invited us to stay at her farm near our ancestral village the weekend of the burial.

"Thank you, Gramma," both Mary and I could well say, "for your final gift of bringing us together."

I liked Mary immediately when I first saw her as an adult, and I could see that most people who knew her liked her, too. Mary is very forthright, honest, and just herself. She is sturdy and slightly shorter than I, has tightly curled dark-blond hair, exudes confidence and speaks her mind with an openness to new ideas, and laughs and swears as heartily as the fair winner in a poker game. I am more tentative and tightly strung, my hair is short and straight and gray, and I sometimes wish to cry at the same things Mary tackles with words or jokes. I am undecided; Mary is not.

In our entire extended family, Mary is the only one who farms for a living, as if she were the branch — the leader — that shot straight up from our dairy-farming trunk. Mary did not choose the trade, however; it chose her.

"I married farming," Mary says.

Her husband, Bill, is a fifth-generation Vermont dairy farmer, working the same land and living in the same homestead as his great-great-grandparents. Farming seized Bill, not from passion for the way of life, but from necessity: His father died, Bill was the only son, and the farm was his widowed mother's livelihood. Suddenly, Bill and Mary, newlyweds who had other professions in mind, were farmers. They were like a sapling tree bent in one direction and then straightened or reversed by a hurricane.

"Farming is hard work," Mary reminds me when I wax sentimental about living on a farm. She and Bill work side-by-side, washing up the pails in the milk room, shoveling manure, and haying in the hot sun. She also juggles with the bankers, cooks continuously, and helps out wherever she is needed.

Mary and I agree we would not have become such good adult friends or revived our childhood sisterlike affection if our husbands had not liked each other so much. It was predictable that they would.

My husband, George, is a dairy farmer, too, at least by upbringing. His parents managed a large dairy farm outside of Chicago in the Fox River Valley where the tilled earth is as rich and dark-looking as chocolate, and the undulating pastures could be a Vermont landscape without the mountains. George started driving the haying tractor when he was nine, as soon as they moved onto the farm, and his older sister, his only sibling, drove the tractor for cultivating corn. They worked right along with the hired hands. I must have known he was a farmer the moment I met him, although he was in professional attire, because I decided immediately that I wished to marry him. His shoulders are slightly bent forward from lugging bales of hay when he was young, like birch limbs permanently pulled over from a winter storm.

George's and Bill's frames are similar. They are each lithe and strong with muscles like a swimmer's. Both men are smart but self-effacing, and they are practical. They also love their families. They remind Mary and me of Grampa.

"Thank you, Grampa, for being such a good model for choosing mates," Mary and I could say.

The evening George and our children and I arrived at Mary's, when our children pretended they were cows coming into her kitchen for dinner, Mary conversed with me while she got dinner ready. She instructed the children to set the table, and she wanted me to listen to something she had on her mind. Apparently some urbanite had criticized the way she and Bill ran their lives.

"I don't care what the busybodies say." Mary spoke firmly as she moved another steaming pot from the stove to drain its water into the sink. "We work hard from five-thirty in the morning until the dishes are done at ten at night. And so we rest hard, too. We take a long nap in the middle of the day except in haying season." Mary moved surely toward dinnertime while she talked.

"See, the busybodies' time for rest might be all weekend and after five each night. The cows don't take vacations to Bermuda or have a wild weekend in Montreal. And neither do we! We rest when we can find the time, and that's usually after lunch. Interrupt Mama Dear when she's snoozing and she might growl," Mary laughed at herself, and the children laughed with her.

"Mama Dear" is Mary's affectionate nickname and "Papa Dear" is Bill's. Mary's sons get in touch with her funny bone by rolling Mama Dear into a plea bargain or using the name to indicate they know she means business. My children call Mary Mama Dear, too, because they know I check in with her on weighty family matters. "Have you called Mama Dear?" they will ask if I seem more anxious or undecided than they can handle. I need reminding that I finally have a sister-cousin-friend, someone I can rely upon who instinctively knows my inner workings.

George had gone out to the barn to help Bill finish milking. The two men came through the kitchen door, and one kicked off his barn boots and the other his dirty new sneakers. They were chuckling about some happening in the barn — an ornery heifer or a varmint in the silo. It all felt so familiar to me, the barn-to-house routine, and I realized that, thirty years later, I had returned to country medicine.

☐

Mary brought to her marriage a dowry that did not come packaged in a box or bank account: our grandparents' farm philosophy. Grampa and Gramma had honed their philosophy from a nineteenth-century agrarian world of routine, hard work, good food, tending family, and rest. They had also accepted the changing world, the twentieth-century industrial pace, with the same equanimity as they had toward the train that ran twice daily along the tracks in their lower field when they ran a dairy farm as big as Bill's and Mary's.

"The whistle blows its long tune about the time I finish milking in the morning and then when I'm about to begin at night," Grampa told me when I was a little girl and he was still milking three cows a day. Grampa said there was little merit in such speed moving through his quiet town. "I never count on it to dictate milking time. Steam engines are just machines, you know, Peanut. No natural inner clock. And they break down."

I am not sure what Grampa understood about human breakdowns, but I recall that he had sympathy for my mother when she was screaming on his back porch during blackberry season the day she was put away. I am told that he was also very good to her when we lived across the street from him during World War II. I would like to talk to Grampa about the other people in my family and my husband's who have broken down, including me, and hear what kind of country medicine he would offer. I do not think he would recommend farming per se as an answer, but maybe he'd suggest resurrecting some of the elements that I have found healing.

"Schools now-a-days should have big windows like the ones I washed and shined," I can imagine Grampa pointing out as one example. "Sunlight, for goodness sake, is something natural and free, and it warms you. It does great things for growing minds, too," he would cheerfully conclude.

My husband's family literally returned to a farm to save his father's health. Theirs is another World War II story about ordinary people who were not fighting on the fronts but were supporting the efforts at home. The Elgin National Watch Company, outside of Chicago, which was renowned for its Swiss movements in clocks and watches, was converted to a defense munitions plant. George's father was a supervisor there, responsible for precision manufacturing of a vital tool: the nose cone that housed the timing fuse for the Mighty Mouse warhead bomb. He was a critical cog in an interlocking gear producing for the war machine. The plant worked around the clock — three swing shifts, day and night — and the product tolerance levels of the vital tool had to be calibrated in thousandths of an inch. Precision, deadlines, warheads, bombs.

George's father's health broke under both the pressure of the work and the knowledge that the bombs meant to strike the enemy could also strike his friends and relatives fighting overseas. He kept on working, but he moved his family out to a relative's farm for the summer where he could get some rest between shifts in a less stressful environment. As luck would have it, at the end of the summer just when his family would have to return to town and he was nearly worn out from doing munitions work, someone from Chicago bought the large dairy farm across the road from his relatives' and hired him as the manager.

"It saved his life," George reflected about his father. "We had a new routine based on animals, not machines. Oh, there were setbacks and variables like the weather or a disease. But nothing's running you out there except nature. Plus, I got to go to a one-room country schoolhouse. It was great!"

When I was thirty-eight, my health broke. Grampa would have said my inner clock was worn out or it could be no longer counted on. Out of all the complicated interlocking reasons for my breakdown, the one that surfaced and stayed in focus until I repaired was my mother. It was a mixture of grief and fear, depression and anxiety. I cried for months and mourned some indescribable loss; and simultaneously, I feared I was going mad like my mother and that I would lose both my sanity and my family as she had done.

My recovery came very slowly, but surely, although I could not measure it at the time. I thought the mental torment would never end. My petit mal had turned into migraines and, finally, under the pressure of denying that the problem might be psychological, my body broke down because I had ignored my head.

"It's all in your head," is the old-fashioned put-down about bodily disorders for which there is no known source. Mine was surely in my head, or my soul.

I was one of the lucky ones in my treatment. First of all, my husband and children never abandoned me. Love is the treatment of choice. My husband was no stranger to breakdowns in his family. Both of his parents had broken down while he was growing up and both survived: They loved each other through the hell. They both had the childhood experience of being orphaned, which surely made each of them sympathetic to the other's needs. Both were placed in the same orphanage, although they did not remember meeting at the time, and then moved from place to place before they met and fell in love. George understood that early childhood losses and constant moving contributed to his parents' feelings of instability, so we agreed that, since moving all my life had caught up with me, we would stay in place, both for my repair and for our children's stability.

The second treatment for my recovery was good outpatient "psyche-work," the hardest work I have ever done. Psychologists do not make house calls; we must go to them. I drove to and from weekly therapy sessions at such a great distance, and for so long, that the sum in miles was equivalent to two and one-half times around the circumference of the earth. I was phobic about driving, so part of the hard work was actually getting to and from the sessions. Phobias, irrational fears of the unknown, are the most excruciatingly painful experiences I have ever known. My psychologist saved my life as surely as if I had been drowning in a great sea and he had leaned over from some boat to pull me out. Except, I had to do my part, seize the helping hand, and struggle to get out. It took years of building strengths from weaknesses, but I finally regained my health.

The third treatment was my return to country medicine, my grandparents' part in my recovery. I might never have remembered their farming philosophy if I had not reconnected with my cousin Mary. Her reappearance in my life brought a personal epiphany of acceptance and truth-telling, the kind of fruit that anyone hopes will appear on their family tree.

It may be the way Mary literally treated me that resurrected my memory of country medicine. She listened when we began talking about matters that lay beneath the surface, and she heard every word plus what was left unsaid. Listening is a great art and a powerful healer. She was the first member of my family of origin to hear my silent cry from childhood.

Then also, Mary is tough. She has the kind of toughness that comes from experience with both nature and human nature with a heavy dose of reality thrown on top. Like our grandparents, she accepts the biblical wisdom that "for every thing there is a season."

"You've had what we call a 'bad season,' " Mary said when I was visiting her once without my family. Mary and I were working on one of the complicated interlocking reasons for my breakdown.

"I'll admit yours has been a long one," she said sympathetically. "But farmers aren't undone by them. We don't give up, and neither have you."

Mary knows all about bad seasons. Farmers are constantly facing some natural setback: droughts, hailstorms, winds, or fires. The bad season Mary and Bill were facing the June when I was visiting was rabies.

"The varmints have come into our territory. We've got to vaccinate all the cows ourselves. Now, this is when Bill says my nursing comes in real handy. And we'll have to kill the barn cats."

"Oh, Mary," I said squeamishly, "how could you?"

"Now, listen," said the leader branch of my family's tree. "There are some things you just have to do to survive. We can't have rabid cats infecting the children around here."

Mary reminded me of our grandparents, the way she accepted and handled realities. Nature and human nature are in a constant dialogue on a farm, I thought.

Mary and Bill and I were the only people on the farm for those few days in June, so they counted on me to do a few light chores. My favorite one was to fetch a gallon of milk from the cow barn because I experienced the essence of country medicine on the short walk: In my heart, I was running to see the Ole Mama Cat in Grampa's barn or following Grampa through the snow tunnel from the barn to home.

From the moment I walk out the kitchen door with the milk can, I am looking at scenery that is peace incarnate for me. Green is everywhere, and in every shade and hue imaginable. There are lawns and raspberry bushes, grapevines and fruit trees, and tall shade trees in the foreground. In the middle-ground are acres of pastureland and a line of hardwoods that mark a stream. The background has a small mountain and a clear blue sky. The path to the pasture runs straight ahead, between a red tractor shed and a big Quonset hay barn, toward a gate. Mary brings the cows through that pasture gate to the milking barn every morning and evening, April through November. The path passes an empty wagon, and then it disappears into the fields of newly planted corn and hay.

I swing the aluminum milk can back and forth as I pass the hay barn. Bill and Mary and their helpers will work the next four months to fill that barn with hay and the silo with silage. I enter the milkroom, which has a wall of sinks and a stainless steel tank as big as a sports car. Milk is running through clear plastic tubing from the cow barn to the tank, and machinery is humming everywhere. In the barn, Holsteins are lined up on both sides of a long, wide, sawdust-covered aisle, and Bill is moving quietly between them as he attaches the milking machinery. A half-dozen tethered calves, with big dark eyes and floppy ears, are either lying or standing in the straw beside the milkroom door. The whole operation smells like fresh, sweet milk. I fill up the milk can from the tank's spigot and slowly walk back to the farmhouse.

While I was soaking up Mama Dear's and Papa Dear's routine for those few days, I felt the pendulum of my inner clock return to measured time the way I must have felt it as a child on our grandparent's farm. There had been a long bad season in my life, but I believed the good alternative was up ahead. I had accepted the given, grieved, and let it go. My natural inner clock was returning back to normal.

□ □ □ □

The Harvest Moon

On a hot and muggy August afternoon in Maine, when I was forty-two, just the age my mother had been when she was put away, I crawled among the blackberry brambles beside our garden and picked a gallon of the wild fruit. I wore overalls, an old long-sleeved shirt, and my mother's red-and-white scarf wrapped around my head.

The scarf is my work hat when I am wallpapering, sawing alders, or berry-picking, but most of all it is my mother's company because I know she wore it when she worked. The scarf is a deep red with little white hearts and is made of rayon, one of those World War II fabrics. It feels cool and soft, although it seems indestructible and it never fades.

When I pick blackberries, I inevitably think about my mother. She had been incommunicado for years, so I remembered the last conversation we had when I was not just talking at her body. My husband and I were visiting with her in the shabby lobby of a now-defunct nursing home. We sat on green or orange plastic saucer-shaped chairs and worked hard at "visiting." My mother had come down the hall, past a dozen drooling or disoriented residents who were strapped in chairs like babies in highchairs, with her purse hanging on her arm as if she had just been shopping and planned to meet old friends at a café. She was dressed in dark blue polyester pants and a thin, worn, gray sweater with lots of pile. I had never before seen her wearing pants. Her attire did not detract, however, from her playing the part of the perfect hostess: polite, ladylike, erect, gracious, and determined to make her guests feel at ease.

She thought I was her sister (so I called her Mattie instead of Mother) and that my husband was just my friend. George engaged her in a conversation about gardening. She was rather wistful about the subject. It was hard to tell if she was talking about a garden she thought she was tending at the time or the one she had tended thirty years before. Their exchange was actually enjoyable to listen to until my husband mentioned something about the Victory Garden he knew she had kept during World War II. The reference reminded Mattie of something painful because she stiffened, lost her smile and wistful gaze, and brought the conversation to a close.

"Putting the garden by is hard work. All that canning. Oh, my, that's no fun." Then she settled the whole business by saying, "I do it all alone."

Mattie opened her big black purse and pulled out a hair brush and comb. Her hair was long, almost all white, healthy-looking, and pulled off her forehead and behind her ears. I remembered when I was a little girl sitting and playing on the floor behind my mother while she brushed her hair before a tall mirror on her dressing table, so I asked if she would like for me to brush her hair.

"Oh, yes, I would," she answered so cheerfully that my offer might have been for refreshments instead of grooming.

My husband watched quietly as Mattie let me brush her locks and fold them over my hand to untangle a small rat's nest with a comb. We did not talk while I worked except for an occasional exchange about the beauty of her hair and her gratitude. Mattie almost did pirouettes in her chair so I could stroke both sides of her head of hair, and I knew this time was both a great privilege and a memory gift to me.

My husband had stood outside the nursing home waiting for me to say my good-byes to Mattie. When I joined him and asked what he was thinking about, he breathed in some fresh air and worked over what I have come to call the three-word epitaph for my mother's life: "What a waste."

☐

Picking berries, I muttered about the thorns and the long tendrils with an almost human will to go their way in spite of my swatting and tugging. I was determined, however, to pick enough to make jelly.

Jelly-making is a rural woman's art. A very successful business-woman in my county prides herself more as a prodigious jelly-maker than as the powerful woman we admire. She polishes the jars, hand-inscribes each label with an imaginative name and the date such as "Gooseberry from Parsons Path '91" or "Fourth of July Elderberry '92," and stocks her floor-to-ceiling jelly cupboard with jams, preserves, conserves, and jelly. Then just before Christmas or deep in the month of February, she beckons guests to her cupboard and gives away her exotic produce.

I was not emulating this successful jelly-maker that afternoon when I set out to gather blackberries and make my own jelly. I was onto something else, although I could not put my finger on the reason at the time.

I crushed the berries in a large stainless-steel pot and stewed the black nubbles until they turned a bricklike red. Then I layered them into a dampened cheesecloth bag, hung it over a big ceramic bread-making bowl in the back hallway, and let it drip so the essence would emerge at the end. The dark juice oozing out of the bag looked like blood. I was happy with my haul and estimated it would make a dozen jars of blackberry jelly in the small antique glasses I had been saving for the project.

Days passed — too many — before I remembered the black-berry juice.

"Aha," I said aloud to no one. "Today's the day. I'll make jelly."

When I lifted the cover off the cream-colored bowl, I found a blue bubbling mass of yeast growing all across the juice and along the inside of the bowl. It was not a few freckles of mold I could skim off and forget. It was rotten to the bottom.

At that moment, something exploded inside of me. Something irrational was happening, and I felt out of control. I paced back and forth in our kitchen and cried and cried. I was angry. I pounded one fist on the counter as I paced across the kitchen, and the other fist as I paced back. I shouted, "How could this happen? How could it? How could it?" My reaction to the spoiled juice was grossly out of proportion to the cause.

Then I knew I had to do something. I picked up the big bowl and held it against my chest. As if parading an offering or a sacrifice, like communion elements in church or a lamb to slaughter, I slowly carried it to the bathroom. I poured the blue-gray, bloody-looking thick juice down the toilet and watched it mix with water. It was purple and disgusting. Feeling sick, I settled to the floor and leaned against the toilet, hugged the bowl, and cried with sobs and screams. I had finally reached some great loss long held within me and flushed the reason for my flood of tears.

"It is all wasted. Just a waste. A half-day to pick and drip the juice, and now no jelly because I forgot. What a waste."

I had broken through a barrier when I flushed the juice. I remembered I had worn my mother's scarf when I picked the berries and that Mattie was put away in August.

"At the same time of the year as right now," I said, amazed. "And she was the age then that I am now." There is a handwritten label on that moment as surely as if I had made and marked the jelly: "Blackberry Season '47."

While I sat crumpled on the bathroom floor, I suddenly remembered my mother stiffening at my husband's question about her Victory Garden. Putting a garden by all alone is hard work, she had said. My mother was under a lot of pressure the summer she broke down. She and my father had been fighting all the time. Plus, it was hot! I remember one afternoon, not long before she was hospitalized in 1947, when my mother was canning with a pressure cooker. I was in the kitchen with her, and suddenly the cooker's top blew off. We were both in the path of the boiling water, and my mother grabbed me, held me, and shook with fright. I form a mental picture of the kitchen explosion as foreshadowing our family upheaval, and my mother's shaking as her premonition of being put away: It was canning season, and she would be shelved for life.

Perhaps I had to reach my mother's age when she was institutionalized before I dared to look at my life without her. I was forty-two and secure in getting well; and when my mother was forty-two, she was just beginning to get worse. The age of forty-two was an apex in both our lives, like the spring and fall equinoxes when the sun crosses the equator and vegetation begins to grow in one hemisphere and lay dormant in the other.

I now know that my intent to berry-pick and make jelly was not simply preparing for some rural woman's art; I was still looking for my mother in the brambles and the season. Whether I had set up the situation unconsciously or had simply forgotten the juice, it does not really matter. I knew when I saw the wasted project that it meant more to me than just lost food. The day I discovered the wasted blackberry juice was my day of reckoning: I had recovered and my mother had not. It was unmercifully unfair. I had to let go of the impossible — that she would somehow miraculously get well — and accept the waste of her life, the failed treatments, the total alienation, and the lack of talk about her. What was there to say?

☐

After I had both come to terms with the truth and repaired from my emotional breakdown, I had two experiences with my mother that might not have occurred without the reckoning: One was a silent bonding, and the other was a cosmic dream.

The bonding experience took place in a nursing home where my mother had just been moved. I had not seen her for a long time, and I had traveled a great distance for the visit. Even after she was pointed out to me in the dining hall and I was wheeling her to her room, I was not at all sure the woman in the wheelchair was my mother. The woman's hair was not as I remembered my mother's when I had combed it, and there was nothing of hers on the dresser or the walls in the room. A nurse and I put the patient into bed, the nurse left, and I still thought there had been some horrible mistake.

The woman before me was mute, so she could not tell me who she was or if I was recognizable to her. She uttered nothing except sounds like a baby's efforts to communicate.

I held her hand and studied her moving facial features. Her cheeks were pink, her nose was familiar. And then I saw her eyes: my mother's eyes. They were light blue, so light that they were white-blue like a thin cloud tinted by the sky.

The bonding was with our eyes. Of course, I thought, we had looked at each other for the first six years of my life while she had fed and bathed and nurtured me. I realized in that moment that, except for my own babies, I had looked into this woman's eyes longer than those of any other human being. I would recognize her anywhere. And, as she responded with the touch of her hand and her willingness to lie still and "talk" by looking, she recognized me, too.

The other experience was what I call a "cosmic dream." For years, I had feared that I would not know when my mother died because she had been moved from place to place without my knowing or assent. Besides the normal need to know when a parent dies, I also wanted desperately to know when her torment was over: It was always on my mind.

I dreamt my cosmic dream on a night when two celestial bodies were prominent in the sky. It was the fullest moon of an equinox — the Harvest Moon in the Northern Hemisphere — and the Planet Mars was the closest to earth it would be for years. My husband and I got up in the early morning hours to view Mars, but what we saw and remembered, because it was so striking, was the profile of a woman bending in the moon. I went back to bed, and it is good I did, because my mother came to me in my dream. She appeared the way the woman in the Harvest Moon had looked, except she was in the Planet Mars, which hung beside the moon behind the tree in our backyard. Mars was circled by a red band, and a great light shone behind it.

I knew the woman in the dream was my mother because the figure was bending like the blue Matisse cutout print that always makes me think of her. The blue woman is half kneeling, and she is bent over with her arm above her head; she looks as if she is working and is burdened. But there is a woman within this woman. The cutout leaves a white space inside the blue woman's enfolding arms and bent body. The space is a profile of a woman sitting straight and tall.

My mother died later that morning. I learned by a telephone call from the nurse who had been with her, but I felt my mother had come to me a few hours before to tell me herself.

I expected to feel a great relief when my mother died, as if the only grief I had to face was her insane life, and that was over. But there was no relief. Instead I felt a great sadness, a sorrow that held both her wasted life and her loss of life. I had more than one loss to grieve at her death, but I did not understand that at the time. My grown daughter comforted me, when I expressed my confusion about how I felt, by saying, "There's no relief, Mom, without grief first."

When we buried Mattie, my husband and our children put a branch of blackberries in her grave. I should have known she would die at the very end of blackberry season, when the harvest is all in and the frost will kill the rest. I added something from the barn we had cleaned out a dozen years before, something I had saved but did not know what for: my mother's calling cards engraved with her married name. Although my parents had been alienated from each other nearly all my life, I knew they once loved each other very much.

There was a light moment afterward when I explained to a friend who did not know my mother why I had put the artifact with her remains.

"Oh," she said with a mixture of sympathy and good humor, "I thought you were just preparing her for a gracious greeting at the Pearly Gates. You said she was a real lady."

Eventually, as my wise daughter had prescribed, my grief over my mother's death did turn to relief. It finally faded as her eyes had paled from light blue to nearly white.

I have two other griefs that her death did not quell. One is over my mother's wasted life. However, as each cycle of the loss returns, something is there to fill it: some natural healing element, a sign or symbol, an image or a place. I have accepted that pattern as the terms of my relationship with my mother, as it has always been and will always be.

The other grief is for growing up, or bringing up, myself. It is for my lost childhood. I sometimes feel it acutely when I am feeding people, and I remember when I was not "fed." Or in raising children, I often lose my way parenting because I want the mothering instead. But my dream the night before my mother died is on call as a memory when I need nurturing myself.

In the dream, the moon and Mars are as near to me as our backyard tree. The Planet Mars is named after the Roman god of war, and my mother's appearance in Mars helps me understand that her war of waste is over. The moon in my dream is bigger than Mars, very bright, devoid of images, and powerful. Since Mars is war, the moon is peace. The Harvest Moon gets its name because it rises just as the sun sets, giving farmers a continuum of light for harvesting. My dream assures me that I have the full moon's strong light helping to fill my emptiness from childhood.

I have learned that dreams are usually products of their dreamers. I gave myself the gift of the Harvest Moon dream. But nature and human nature had given me the symbols: an ancient one of war and one of peace. There was something almost seasonal about the timing of my mother's death and my reckoning, like the spring and fall equinoxes when the sun crosses the equator and one hemisphere's vegetation becomes dormant while the other one is quickening. I dare to say, as I draw on the image of planets in their courses, that my soul was at the right part of its ellipse to have had the Harvest Moon dream at all.

My mother's and my life had been a whole, although we were apart, like the two hemispheres under the same moon. There is a season for every thing under heaven, I thought —a time to mourn, and a time to heal.

H.H.PRICE, a native of Vermont, is a writer who lives in Maine. Her essays have appeared in *Vermont Life, Gourmet,* and *Country Journal.*

Blackberry Season is her first book. It is a true story, drawn from her own life situation.

She received her B.A. from Northwestern University, Evanston, Illinois, where she studied the History and Literature of World Religions. She also studied with H. Westman, a pioneer in the theory and practice of psychotherapy.

Harriet and her husband have lived and worked in Maine since 1969. They have two adult children.

Other LuraMedia Publications

BANKSON, MARJORY ZOET

Braided Streams:
Esther and a Woman's Way of Growing

Seasons of Friendship:
Naomi and Ruth as a Pattern

"This Is My Body. . .":
Creativity, Clay, and Change

BOHLER, CAROLYN STAHL

Prayer on Wings: *A Search for Authentic Prayer*

DOHERTY, DOROTHY ALBRACHT
and McNAMARA, MARY COLGAN

Out of the Skin Into the Soul:
The Art of Aging

GEIGER, LURA JANE

and PATRICIA BACKMAN
Braided Streams Leader's Guide

and SUSAN TOBIAS
Seasons of Friendship Leader's Guide

JEVNE, RONNA FAY

It All Begins With Hope:
Patients, Caretakers, and the Bereaved Speak Out

and ALEXANDER LEVITAN

No Time for Nonsense:
Getting Well Against the Odds

KEIFFER, ANN

Gift of the Dark Angel: *A Woman's Journey
through Depression toward Wholeness*

LODER, TED

Eavesdropping on the Echoes:
Voices from the Old Testament

Guerrillas of Grace:
Prayers for the Battle

Tracks in the Straw:
Tales Spun from the Manger

Wrestling the Light:
Ache and Awe in the Human-Divine Struggle

MEYER, RICHARD C.

One Anothering:
Biblical Building Blocks for Small Groups

MILLETT, CRAIG

In God's Image:
Archetypes of Women in Scripture

O'CONNOR, ELIZABETH

Search for Silence *(Revised Edition)*

PRICE, H.H.

Blackberry Season:
A Time to Mourn, A Time to Heal

RAFFA, JEAN BENEDICT

The Bridge to Wholeness:
A Feminine Alternative to the Hero Myth

SAURO, JOAN

Whole Earth Meditation:
Ecology for the Spirit

SCHAPER, DONNA

Stripping Down:
The Art of Spiritual Restoration

WEEMS, RENITA J.

Just a Sister Away: *A Womanist Vision
of Women's Relationships in the Bible*

The Women's Series

BORTON, JOAN

Drawing from the Women's Well:
Reflections on the Life Passage of Menopause

CARTLEDGE-HAYES, MARY

To Love Delilah:
Claiming the Women of the Bible

DUERK, JUDITH

Circle of Stones:
Woman's Journey to Herself

**O'HALLORAN, SUSAN and
DELATTRE, SUSAN**

The Woman Who Lost Her Heart:
A Tale of Reawakening

RUPP, JOYCE

The Star in My Heart:
Experiencing Sophia, Inner Wisdom

SCHNEIDER-AKER, KATHERINE

God's Forgotten Daughter:
*A Modern Midrash: What If
Jesus Had Been A Woman?*

LuraMedia, Inc. , 7060 Miramar Rd., Suite 104, San Diego, CA 92121
Call 1-800-FOR-LURA for information about bookstores or ordering.
Books for Healing and Hope, Balance and Justice.